STORY WRITING WINGS 02
Symphony

STORY WRITING WINGS 02
Symphony

초판 1쇄 발행	2008년 10월 21일
지은이	한일
감 수	Ryan Goessl
펴낸이	신성현, 오상욱
만든이	남영림, 성경모, 윤은아
펴낸곳	도서출판 아이엠북스
	153-802 서울시 금천구 가산동 327-32 대륭테크노타운 12차 1116호
	Tel. (02)6343-0997~9 Fax. (02)6343-0995
출판등록	2006년 6월 7일 제 313-2006-000122호
출판등록	2006년 6월 7일 제 313-2006-000122호
내지 디자인	디자인 디도
표지 디자인	안성민
ISBN	978-89-92334-60-0 (14740)

저자와의 협의에 따라 인지는 붙이지 않습니다.
잘못된 책은 구입하신 곳에서 교환해 드립니다.
이 책에 게재된 내용의 일부 또는 전체를 무단으로 복제 및 발췌하는 것을 금합니다.

www.iambooks.co.kr

STORY WRITING WINGS 02
Symphony

한일 지음

CONTENTS

What is the Story Writing? 6
Construction & Character 8

Unit 1 목적어와 보어 12
    Grammar
    Sentences with Grammar
    Story Writing-Paragraph 1
    Story Writing-Paragraph 2
    Story Writing-Paragraph 3
    Error Analysis

Unit 2 형용사의 한정적 용법 24
    Grammar
    Sentences with Grammar
    Story Writing-Paragraph 1
    Story Writing-Paragraph 2
    Story Writing-Paragraph 3
    Error Analysis

Unit 3 현재분사 vs 과거분사 40
    Grammar
    Sentences with Grammar
    Story Writing-Paragraph 1
    Story Writing-Paragraph 2
    Story Writing-Paragraph 3
    Error Analysis

Unit 4 전치사구의 형용사적 용법   52
    Grammar
    Sentences with Grammar
    Story Writing-Paragraph 1
    Story Writing-Paragraph 2
    Story Writing-Paragraph 3
    Error Analysis

Unit 5 합성전치사   64
    Grammar
    Sentences with Grammar
    Story Writing-Paragraph 1
    Story Writing-Paragraph 2
    Story Writing-Paragraph 3
    Error Analysis

Unit 6 합성전치사의 강조   78
    Grammar
    Sentences with Grammar
    Story Writing-Paragraph 1
    Story Writing-Paragraph 2
    Story Writing-Paragraph 3
    Error Analysis

Writing Guideline   93

What is the Story Writing?

하나의 문장이 만들어지기 위해서는 반드시 그 시작점이 있습니다. 영어도 마찬가지입니다. 영어는 두 개의 단어로 문장을 시작합니다.

> I buy.
> 주어 동사
> He comes.
> 주어 동사
> They study.
> 주어 동사
> We clean.
> 주어 동사

Story Writing은 문장이 만들어지는 가장 기본적인 시작점, 즉 두 개의 단어를 시작점으로 출발하여 한편의 Story를 만들어갑니다.

하나의 문장이 두 개의 단어로 출발하여 어떠한 문법적인 경로를 통해서 길어지는가, 또 각각의 문법들은 서로 어떠한 경로를 통해서 구조적으로 긴밀하게 연결되는가, 그렇게 상호 긴밀히 연결된 문법들이 글의 내용과 수준에 어떠한 영향을 미치는가에 대하여 한편의 Story를 완성시켜가며 살펴보게 됩니다.

처음에는 두 개의 단어로 구성된 20~30분 분량의 짧은 Story를 만나게 됩니다. 이후 짧은 Story가 길어지기 위해서 필요한 문법들을 만나고, Story의 구조도 더욱 정교해지며, 전달하고자 하는 내용도 자세해지는 과정을 겪게 됩니다.

이 책에서 Unit 1-Story는 Unit 2-Story를 쓸 수 있는 바탕을 마련해줍니다. 또한, Unit 1, 2의 Story는 Unit 3-Story를 쓸 수 있는 바탕을 마련해 줍니다.

각각의 Unit에서 Story가 더해갈수록 글의 길이는 길어지고, 요구되는 문법도 복잡해집니다. 단계별로 문법적 요소를 첨가해가면, 구조적으로 풍부한 한편의 Story를 완성하게 되고, 2시간 분량의 Story를 쓸 수 있는 능력을 키우도록 도와줍니다.

Story Writing에서 문법을 요구하는 이유는 Writing과 문법과의 긴밀한 연결 관계를 느끼게 하기 위해서입니다. Unit과 함께 길어지는 Story에 요구되는 문법을 차례대로 공부하다 보면 문법에도 어떠한 문법이 먼저이고, 어떠한 문법이 나중인지, 문법에도 순서가 있음을 느끼게 될 것입니다.

각 Unit의 Story를 쓰기 위해서 실생활에서 사용 비중이 높은 문법들이 소개되어 있습니다.

여러분은 Story Writing에서 단지 Writing에만 집중할 것이 아니라, 각각의 Unit마다 제시된 문법과도 친숙해 지기를 바랍니다.

Story Writing의 가장 큰 장점은 영어문장을 체계적으로 바라볼 수 있는 시야를 지닌다는 것입니다. 영어문장을 체계적으로 관리할 수 있는 능력은 바로 Writing과 Reading에 직접적인 영향을 끼칩니다.

Story Writing을 통해 여러분은 결국 2시간 이상의 Writing을 할 수 있는 능력을 가지게 될 것입니다. 또한 Story가 어떠한 문법적인 경로를 통해 길어졌는지를 알 수 있다면, 여러분은 틀림없이 어떠한 Writing이라도 할 수 있다는 자신감을 가지게 될 것입니다.

Grammar

Story Writing에 필요한 문법을 소개합니다.

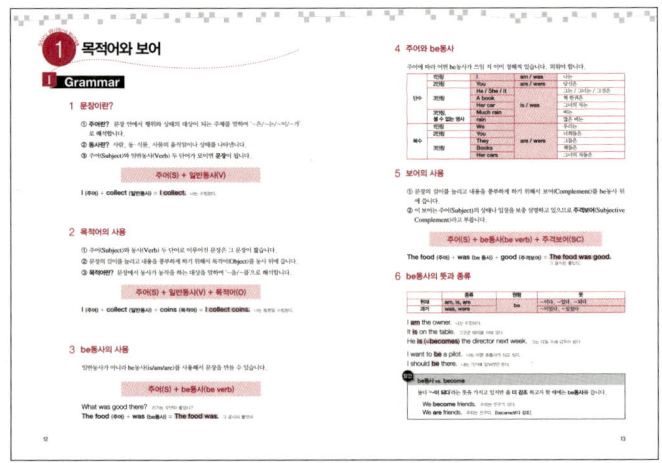

Sentences with Grammar

앞서 배운 핵심 문법을 이해하며 약 20개의 **문장쓰기 연습**을 해 봅니다. 이 문장들은 뒤이어 나올 Story Writing을 좀 더 자연스럽게 할 수 있도록 적절한 어휘 선택을 도와줍니다.

Story Writing

문장쓰기 → 문단쓰기 → **Story** 완성.
각 Unit은 3개의 문단(paragraph)으로 구성된 하나의 Story를 완성하기 위하여, 문단을 구성 할 문장들을 차근차근 만들어 보도록 합니다. 결국 3개의 문단이 만들어지고 한 개의 Story가 완성됩니다. 각 Unit이 끝날 때마다 하나의 Story가 완성되지만, Unit이 올라갈수록 다양한 문법을 익힘과 동시에 같은 Story이지만 내용이 더 풍부해지고 길어지게 됩니다.

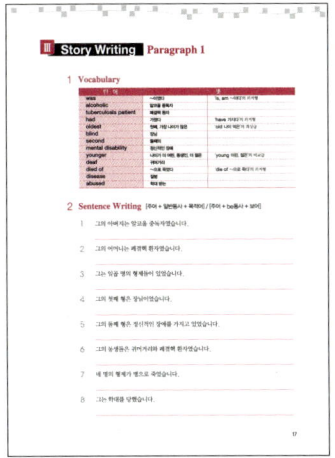
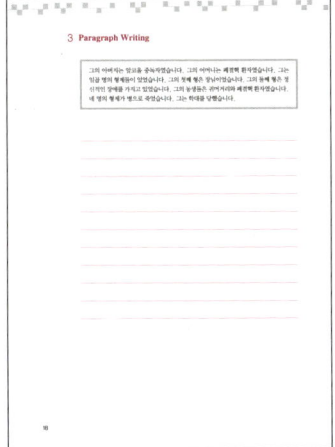

Error Analysis

각 Unit에서 익힌 문법, 표현과 Story의 내용을 상기하면서 Story안에 **틀린 부분을 찾아** 고칩니다.

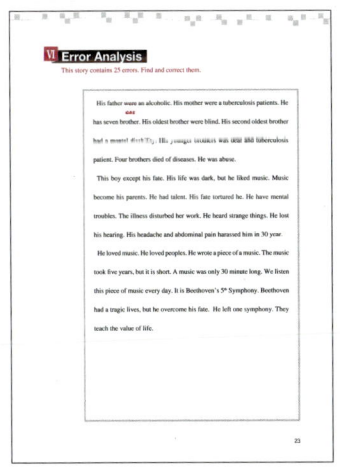

Rewriting

문법공부를 위해 만들어진 Story는 내용이 부자연스러워질 수 있습니다. 그러므로, 문법보다는 내용이 자연스러워 지도록 Rewriting한 Story를 이 부분에서 소개하고 있습니다.

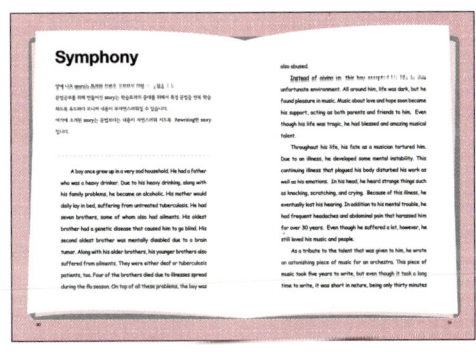

Story Writing Wings 02

Symphony

Contents

Unit 1 목적어와 보어
Unit 2 형용사의 한정적 용법
Unit 3 현재분사 vs 과거분사
Unit 4 전치사구의 형용사적 용법
Unit 5 합성전치사
Unit 6 합성전치사와 접속

1 목적어와 보어

I Grammar

1 문장이란?

① **주어란?** 문장 안에서 행위와 상태의 대상이 되는 주체를 말하며 '~은/~는/~이/~가'로 해석합니다.
② **동사란?** 사람, 동·식물, 사물의 움직임이나 상태를 나타냅니다.
③ 주어(Subject)와 일반동사(Verb) 두 단어가 모이면 **문장**이 됩니다.

> **주어(S) + 일반동사(V)**

I (주어) + collect (일반동사) = **I collect.**   나는 수집한다.

2 목적어의 사용

① 주어(Subject)와 동사(Verb) 두 단어로 이루어진 문장은 그 문장이 짧습니다.
② 문장의 길이를 늘리고 내용을 풍부하게 하기 위해서 목적어(Object)를 동사 뒤에 씁니다.
③ **목적어란?** 문장에서 동사가 동작을 하는 대상을 말하며 '~을/~를'으로 해석합니다.

> **주어(S) + 일반동사(V) + 목적어(O)**

I (주어) + collect (일반동사) + coins (목적어) = **I collect coins.**   나는 동전을 수집한다.

3 be동사의 사용

일반동사가 아니라 be동사(is/am/are)를 사용해서 문장을 만들 수 있습니다.

> **주어(S) + be동사(be verb)**

What was good there?   거기는 무엇이 좋았니?
The food (주어) + **was** (be동사) = **The food was.**   그 음식이 좋았어.

4 주어와 be동사

주어에 따라 어떤 be동사가 쓰일 지 이미 정해져 있습니다. 외워야 합니다.

단수	1인칭	I	am / was	나는
	2인칭	You	are / were	당신은
	3인칭	He / She / It	is / was	그는 / 그녀는 / 그것은
		A book		책 한권은
		Her car		그녀의 차는
	3인칭, 셀 수 없는 명사	Rain		비는
		Much rain		많은 비는
복수	1인칭	We	are / were	우리는
	2인칭	You		너희들은
	3인칭	They		그들은
		Books		책들은
		Her cars		그녀의 차들은

5 보어의 사용

① 문장의 길이를 늘리고 내용을 풍부하게 하기 위해서 보어(Complement)를 be동사 뒤에 씁니다.
② 이 보어는 주어(Subject)의 상태나 입장을 보충 설명하고 있으므로 **주격보어**(Subjective Complement)라고 부릅니다.

주어(S) + be동사(be verb) + 주격보어(SC)

The food (주어) + was (be 동사) + good (주격보어) = **The food was good.**
그 음식은 좋았다.

6 be동사의 뜻과 종류

	종류	원형	뜻
현재	am, is, are	be	~이다, ~있다, ~되다
과거	was, were		~이었다, ~있었다

I **am** the owner. 나는 주인이다.
It **is** on the table. 그것은 테이블 위에 있다.
He **is** (=**becomes**) the director next week. 그는 다음주에 감독이 된다.
I want to **be** a pilot. 나는 비행기 조종사가 되고 싶다.
I should **be** there. 나는 거기에 있어야만 한다.

 be동사 vs. become

둘다 '~**이 되다**'라는 뜻을 가지고 있지만 좀 **더 강조** 하고자 할 때에는 **be동사**를 씁니다.

We **become** friends. 우리는 친구가 되다.
We **are** friends. 우리는 친구다. [become보다 강조]

II. Sentences with Grammar

[주어 + 일반동사 + 목적어] / [주어 + be동사 + 보어]

1. 그 지원자는 대표자가 되었다.

   ▶ _____

   Word Tips volunteer, representative

2. 그 여자가 그 관리자였다.

   ▶ _____

   Word Tips controller

3. 그 학생은 영리했다.

   ▶ _____

   Word Tips smart

4. 그 손님들은 까다로웠다.

   ▶ _____

   Word Tips customers, picky

5. 모두가 그 제안을 받아들였다.

   ▶ _____

   Word Tips accepted, suggestion

6. 사람들은 그 맛을 좋아했다.

   ▶ _____

   Word Tips liked, taste

7 그 건물은 큰 시계를 가지고 있다.

▶ _____
Word Tips has, clock

8 그 가려움증은 나를 괴롭혔다.

▶ _____
Word Tips itching, tortured

9 그 잡음은 나의 집중력을 방해했다.

▶ _____
Word Tips noises, disturbed, concentration

10 나의 남동생은 무엇인가를 만들었다.

▶ _____
Word Tips something

11 한 승객이 그의 여권을 잃어버렸다.

▶ _____
Word Tips passenger, lost

12 그의 잔소리는 일하는 사람들을 괴롭혔다.

▶ _____
Word Tips scolding, harassed

13 그 미술 선생님은 종이 한 장을 준비했다.

▶ _____
Word Tips art, prepared, a piece of

14 그 공사는 11년이나 걸렸다.
▶ _____
Word Tips construction, took

15 그의 연설은 28초였다.
▶ _____
Word Tips speech

16 그 참가자들은 소식을 들었다.
▶ _____
Word Tips participants, listened to

17 그 경치는 장관이다.
▶ _____
Word Tips view, sublime

18 그 도전자는 그의 단점을 극복했다.
▶ _____
Word Tips overcame, shortcomings

19 그녀의 마지막 말이 여운을 남겼다.
▶ _____
Word Tips words, left, suggestiveness

20 이 책은 운동의 중요성을 가르친다.
▶ _____
Word Tips importance, exercise

III. Story Writing　Paragraph 1

1　Vocabulary

단 어		뜻
was	~이였다	'is, am ~이다'의 과거형
alcoholic	알코올 중독자	
tuberculosis patient	폐결핵 환자	
had	가졌다	'have 가지다'의 과거형
oldest	첫째, 가장 나이가 많은	'old 나이 먹은'의 최상급
blind	장님	
second	둘째의	
mental disability	정신적인 장애	
younger	나이가 더 어린, 동생인, 더 젊은	'young 어린, 젊은'의 비교급
deaf	귀머거리	
died of	~으로 죽었다	'die of ~으로 죽다'의 과거형
disease	질병	
abused	학대 받는	

2　Sentence Writing　[주어 + 일반동사 + 목적어] / [주어 + be동사 + 보어]

1　그의 아버지는 알코올 중독자였습니다.

2　그의 어머니는 폐결핵 환자였습니다.

3　그는 일곱 명의 형제들이 있었습니다.

4　그의 첫째 형은 장님이었습니다.

5　그의 둘째 형은 정신적인 장애를 가지고 있었습니다.

6　그의 동생들은 귀머거리와 폐결핵 환자였습니다.

7　네 명의 형제가 병으로 죽었습니다.

8　그는 학대를 당했습니다.

3 Paragraph Writing

> 그의 아버지는 알코올 중독자였습니다. 그의 어머니는 폐결핵 환자였습니다. 그는 일곱 명의 형제들이 있었습니다. 그의 첫째 형은 장님이었습니다. 그의 둘째 형은 정신적인 장애를 가지고 있었습니다. 그의 동생들은 귀머거리와 폐결핵 환자였습니다. 네 명의 형제가 병으로 죽었습니다. 그는 학대를 당했습니다.

IV Story Writing   Paragraph 2

1 Vocabulary

단 어	뜻	단 어	뜻	
fate	운명	accepted	받아들였다	accept의 과거형
life	삶, 생활	tortured	괴롭혔다	torture의 과거형
talent	재능	disturbed	방해했다	disturb의 과거형
illness	병	strange things	이상한 소리, 헛소리	
hearing	청력	lost	잃어버렸다	lose의 과거형
headache	두통, 머리아픔	harassed	괴롭혔다	harass의 과거형
abdominal	복부의, 아랫배의	mental troubles	정신병	

2 Sentence Writing   [주어 + 일반동사 + 목적어] / [주어 + be동사 + 보어]

1 이 소년은 그의 운명을 받아들였습니다.

2 그의 삶은 어두웠지만, 그는 음악을 좋아했습니다.

3 음악이 그의 부모가 되었습니다.

4 그는 재능을 가지고 있었습니다.

5 그의 운명은 그를 괴롭혔습니다.

6 그는 정신병에 걸렸습니다.

7 그 병은 그의 일을 방해했습니다.

8 그는 헛소리를 들었습니다.

9 그는 그의 청력을 잃어버렸습니다.

10 그의 두통과 복통은 30년간 그를 괴롭혔습니다.

3 Paragraph Writing

이 소년은 그의 운명을 받아들였습니다. 그의 삶은 어두웠지만, 그는 음악을 좋아했습니다. 음악이 그의 부모가 되었습니다. 그는 재능을 가지고 있었습니다. 그의 운명은 그를 괴롭혔습니다. 그는 정신병에 걸렸습니다. 그 병은 그의 일을 방해했습니다. 그는 헛소리를 들었습니다. 그는 그의 청력을 잃어버렸습니다. 그의 두통과 복통은 30년간 그를 괴롭혔습니다.

Ⅴ Story Writing — Paragraph 3

1 Vocabulary

단 어	뜻	단 어	뜻
a piece of	~의 한 곡, ~의 한 조각	wrote	썼다, 작성했다	write의 과거형
short	짧은	took	(시간이) ~걸렸다	take의 과거형
only	단지, 오직	~ minutes long	길이가 ~분	
listen to	~을 듣다	Beethoven's 5th Symphony	베토벤 5번 교향곡	
every day	매일	overcame	극복했다	overcome의 과거형
tragic	비극적인, 비운의	left	남겼다	leave의 과거형
value of	~의 가치	teaches	가르치다	teach의 3인칭 단수형

2 Sentence Writing [주어 + 일반동사 + 목적어] / [주어 + be동사 + 보어]

1. 그는 음악을 사랑했습니다.

2. 그는 사람들을 사랑했습니다.

3. 그는 곡을 하나 썼습니다.

4. 그 곡은 5년이 걸렸지만, 그것은 짧았습니다.

5. 그 곡은 길이가 단지 30분이었습니다.

6. 우리는 이 곡을 매일 듣습니다.

7. 그것은 베토벤 5번 교향곡입니다.

8. 베토벤은 비극적인 삶을 가지고 있었지만, 그는 그의 운명을 극복했습니다.

9. 그는 하나의 교향곡을 남겼습니다.

10. 그것은 삶의 가치를 가르쳐줍니다.

3 Paragraph Writing

> 그는 음악을 사랑했습니다. 그는 사람들을 사랑했습니다. 그는 곡을 하나 썼습니다. 그 곡은 5년이나 걸렸습니다. 하지만 그것은 짧았습니다. 그 곡은 길이가 단지 30분이었습니다. 우리는 이 곡을 매일 듣습니다. 그것은 베토벤 5번 교향곡입니다. 베토벤은 비극적인 삶을 가지고 있었지만, 그는 그의 운명을 극복했습니다. 그는 하나의 교향곡을 남겼습니다. 그것은 삶의 가치를 가르쳐줍니다.

VI Error Analysis

This story contains 25 errors. Find and correct them.

His father ~~were~~ an alcoholic. His mother were a tuberculosis patients. He
was
has seven brothers. His oldest brother were blind. His second oldest brother had a mental disability. His younger brothers was deaf and tuberculosis patient. Four brothers died of diseases. He was abuse.

This boy except his fate. His life was dark, but he liked music. Music become his parents. He had talent. His fate tortured he. He have mental troubles. The illness disturbed her work. He heard strange things. He lost his hearing. His headache and abdominal pain harassed him in 30 year.

He loved music. He loved peoples. He wrote a piece of a music. The music took five years, but it is short. A music was only 30 minute long. We listen this piece of music every day. It is Beethoven's 5th Symphony. Beethoven had a tragic lives, but he overcome his fate. He left one symphony. They teach the value of life.

2 형용사의 한정적 용법

I Grammar

1 형용사란?

① 사람, 동·식물, 사물의 성질이나 상태를 나타냅니다.
② 주로 명사 앞에 놓여 그 명사를 설명해줍니다. 좀 더 어려운 말로 '명사를 수식한다'고 말하기도 합니다.
③ 형용사가 명사 앞에 놓여 그 명사를 수식하는 것을 **형용사의 한정적 용법** 또는 **제한적 용법**이라고 말합니다.

형용사의 한정적 용법	형용사(Adjective) + 명사(Noun)

important vocabulary 중요한 어휘   **cute** boys 귀여운 소년들

cold water 차가운 물   **blue** eyes 파란 눈

2 형용사와 문장의 level

① 형용사는 문장의 level을 정하는데 중요한 요소로도 사용이 됩니다.
② 어떤 형용사를 사용하는지에 따라 글의 level을 달리 할 수 있습니다.

[Level 1] **good** ideas 좋은 생각들   I have **good** ideas.
[Level 2] **helpful** ideas 도움이 되는 생각들   I have **helpful** ideas.
[Level 3] **innovative** ideas 혁신적인 생각들   I have **innovative** ideas.

[Level 1] a **bad** situation 나쁜 상황   It is a **bad** situation.
[Level 2] a **serious** situation 심각한 상황   It is a **serious** situation.
[Level 3] a **critical** situation 중대한 상황   It is a **critical** situation.

[Level 1] **nice** rooms 좋은 방들   They have **nice** rooms.
[Level 2] **clean** rooms 깨끗한 방들   They have **clean** rooms.
[Level 3] **comfortable** rooms 편안한 방들   They have **comfortable** rooms.

3 많이 쓰이는 형용사들

다음은 생활에서 자주 사용되는 형용사들이므로 외워 두는 것이 좋습니다. 각 형용사의 뜻을 적어 보면서 차근차근 외워 보도록 하세요.

abundant	_____	brief	_____
adorable	_____	bright	_____
adventurous	_____	broad	_____
aggressive	_____	broken	_____
agreeable	_____	bumpy	_____
alert	_____	busy	_____
alive	_____	calm	_____
amused	_____	careful	_____
ancient	_____	cautious	_____
angry	_____	charming	_____
annoyed	_____	cheerful	_____
annoying	_____	chilly	_____
anxious	_____	chubby	_____
arrogant	_____	clean	_____
ashamed	_____	clear	_____
attractive	_____	clever	_____
average	_____	cloudy	_____
awful	_____	clumsy	_____
bad	_____	cold	_____
beautiful	_____	colorful	_____
better	_____	colossal	_____
bewildered	_____	combative	_____
big	_____	comfortable	_____
bitter	_____	concerned	_____
black	_____	condemned	_____
bloody	_____	confused	_____
blue	_____	cooing	_____
blushing	_____	cool	_____
boiling	_____	cooperative	_____
bored	_____	courageous	_____
brainy	_____	crazy	_____
brave	_____	creepy	_____
breakable	_____	crooked	_____
breezy	_____	crowded	_____

cruel	_____	encouraging	_____
cuddly	_____	energetic	_____
curious	_____	enthusiastic	_____
curly	_____	envious	_____
curved	_____	evil	_____
cute	_____	excited	_____
damaged	_____	expensive	_____
damp	_____	exuberant	_____
dangerous	_____	faint	_____
dark	_____	fair	_____
dead	_____	faithful	_____
deafening	_____	famous	_____
deep	_____	fancy	_____
defeated	_____	fantastic	_____
defiant	_____	fast	_____
delicious	_____	fat	_____
delightful	_____	few	_____
depressed	_____	fierce	_____
determined	_____	filthy	_____
different	_____	fine	_____
difficult	_____	flaky	_____
dirty	_____	flat	_____
disgusted	_____	fluffy	_____
distinct	_____	fluttering	_____
disturbed	_____	foolish	_____
dizzy	_____	fragile	_____
doubtful	_____	frail	_____
drab	_____	frantic	_____
dry	_____	freezing	_____
dull	_____	fresh	_____
dusty	_____	friendly	_____
eager	_____	frightened	_____
early	_____	funny	_____
easy	_____	fuzzy	_____
elated	_____	gentle	_____
elegant	_____	gifted	_____
embarrassed	_____	gigantic	_____
empty	_____	glamorous	_____
enchanting	_____	gleaming	_____

glorious	_____	inquisitive	_____
good	_____	itchy	_____
gorgeous	_____	jealous	_____
graceful	_____	jittery	_____
greasy	_____	jolly	_____
great	_____	joyous	_____
grieving	_____	juicy	_____
grotesque	_____	kind	_____
grubby	_____	large	_____
grumpy	_____	late	_____
handsome	_____	lazy	_____
happy	_____	light	_____
hard	_____	little	_____
harsh	_____	lively	_____
healthy	_____	lonely	_____
heavy	_____	long	_____
helpful	_____	loose	_____
helpless	_____	loud	_____
high	_____	lovely	_____
high-pitched	_____	low	_____
hilarious	_____	lucky	_____
hissing	_____	magnificent	_____
hollow	_____	mammoth	_____
homeless	_____	many	_____
homely	_____	massive	_____
horrible	_____	melodic	_____
hot	_____	melted	_____
huge	_____	miniature	_____
hungry	_____	misty	_____
hurt	_____	moaning	_____
hushed	_____	modern	_____
husky	_____	motionless	_____
icy	_____	muddy	_____
ill	_____	mushy	_____
immense	_____	mute	_____
important	_____	mysterious	_____
impossible	_____	narrow	_____
inexpensive	_____	nasty	_____
innocent	_____	naughty	_____

nervous	_____	rich	_____
nice	_____	ripe	_____
noisy	_____	rotten	_____
numerous	_____	rough	_____
nutritious	_____	round	_____
nutty	_____	salty	_____
obedient	_____	scary	_____
obnoxious	_____	scattered	_____
odd	_____	scrawny	_____
old	_____	screeching	_____
old-fashioned	_____	selfish	_____
open	_____	shaggy	_____
outrageous	_____	shaky	_____
outstanding	_____	shallow	_____
panicky	_____	sharp	_____
perfect	_____	shiny	_____
petite	_____	shivering	_____
plain	_____	short	_____
plastic	_____	shrill	_____
pleasant	_____	shy	_____
poised	_____	silent	_____
poor	_____	silky	_____
powerful	_____	silly	_____
precious	_____	skinny	_____
prickly	_____	sleepy	_____
proud	_____	slimy	_____
puny	_____	slippery	_____
purring	_____	slow	_____
puzzled	_____	small	_____
quaint	_____	smiling	_____
quick	_____	smoggy	_____
quiet	_____	smooth	_____
rainy	_____	soft	_____
rapid	_____	solid	_____
raspy	_____	sore	_____
real	_____	sour	_____
relieved	_____	sparkling	_____
repulsive	_____	spicy	_____
resonant	_____	splendid	_____

spotless	_____	tiny	_____
square	_____	tired	_____
squealing	_____	tough	_____
stale	_____	troubled	_____
steady	_____	ugly	_____
steep	_____	uneven	_____
sticky	_____	uninterested	_____
stormy	_____	unsightly	_____
straight	_____	unusual	_____
strange	_____	upset	_____
strong	_____	uptight	_____
stupid	_____	vast	_____
substantial	_____	victorious	_____
successful	_____	vivacious	_____
super	_____	voiceless	_____
sweet	_____	wandering	_____
swift	_____	warm	_____
talented	_____	weak	_____
tall	_____	weary	_____
tame	_____	wet	_____
tart	_____	whispering	_____
tasteless	_____	wicked	_____
tasty	_____	wide	_____
teeny	_____	wide-eyed	_____
tender	_____	wild	_____
tense	_____	witty	_____
terrible	_____	wonderful	_____
testy	_____	wooden	_____
thankful	_____	worried	_____
thirsty	_____	wrong	_____
thoughtful	_____	young	_____
thoughtless	_____	yummy	_____
thundering	_____	zany	_____
tight	_____	zealous	_____

Keep ans Share (2004). Group sharing made easy and secure. Adjective list, Retrieved October 10, 2008 from the World Wide Web: http://www.adjectives-list.com

II. Sentences with Grammar

[형용사의 한정적용법]

1. 그 지원자는 **중요한** 대표자가 되었다.

   ▶ _____

   Word Tips important

2. 그 여자가 그 **엄격한** 관리자였다.

   ▶ _____

   Word Tips strict

3. 그 **새로 온** 학생은 영리했다.

   ▶ _____

   Word Tips new

4. 그 **외국** 손님들은 까다로웠다.

   ▶ _____

   Word Tips foreign, picky

5. 모두가 그 **합당한** 제안을 받아들였다.

   ▶ _____

   Word Tips reasonable

6. **어떤** 사람들은 그 맛을 좋아했다.

   ▶ _____

   Word Tips some

7 그 건물은 크고 **화려한** 시계를 가지고 있다.

▶ _____

Word Tips and, gorgeous

8 그 **심한** 가려움증은 나를 괴롭혔다.

▶ _____

Word Tips severe, tortured

9 그 **끊임없이 계속되는** 잡음은 나의 집중력을 방해했다.

▶ _____

Word Tips constant, disturbed, concentration

10 나의 **영리한** 남동생은 무엇인가를 만들었다.

▶ _____

Word Tips smart

11 한 **남성** 승객이 그의 여권을 잃어버렸다.

▶ _____

Word Tips male, lost

12 그의 **시시콜콜한** 잔소리는 일하는 사람들을 괴롭혔다.

▶ _____

Word Tips inquisitive, harassed

13 그 미술 선생님은 **파란** 종이 한 장을 준비했다.

▶ _____

Word Tips a piece of, blue

14 그 **위험한** 공사는 11년이나 걸렸다.

   ▶ _____
   Word Tips dangerous

15 그의 **강한 인상을 주는** 연설은 28초였다.

   ▶ _____
   Word Tips powerful

16 그 참가자들은 **중요한** 소식을 들었다.

   ▶ _____
   Word Tips listened to, important

17 그 **숨막힐 듯한** 경치는 장관이다.

   ▶ _____
   Word Tips breathtaking, sublime

18 그 **위대한** 도전자는 그의 단점을 극복했다.

   ▶ _____
   Word Tips great, overcame

19 그녀의 마지막 말이 **강한** 여운을 남겼다.

   ▶ _____
   Word Tips strong, suggestiveness

20 이 책은 운동의 **참된** 중요성을 가르친다.

   ▶ _____
   Word Tips true, importance

III. Story Writing Paragraph 1

1 Vocabulary

단 어	뜻	단 어	뜻
abusive	학대하는	deaf	귀머거리
alcoholic	알코올 중독자	fatal	치명적인, 생명에 영향을 주는
serious	심각한	died of	~으로 죽었다
born blind	태어날 때부터 장님, 타고난 장님	incurable	불치의

2 Sentence Writing [형용사의 한정적용법]

1 그의 **학대하는** 아버지는 알코올 중독자였습니다.

2 그의 어머니는 **심각한** 폐결핵 환자였습니다.

3 그는 일곱 명의 형제들이 있었습니다.

4 그의 첫째 형은 **타고난** 장님이었습니다.

5 그의 둘째 형은 정신적인 장애를 가지고 있었습니다.

6 그의 동생들은 귀머거리와 **치명적인** 폐결핵 환자였습니다.

7 네 명의 형제가 **불치의** 병으로 죽었습니다.

8 그는 학대를 당했습니다.

3 Paragraph Writing

> 그의 **학대하는** 아버지는 알코올 중독자였습니다. 그의 어머니는 **심각한** 폐결핵 환자였습니다. 그는 일곱 명의 형제들이 있었습니다. 그의 첫째 형은 **타고난** 장님이었습니다. 그의 둘째 형은 정신적인 장애를 가지고 있었습니다. 그의 동생들은 귀머거리와 **치명적인** 폐결핵 환자였습니다. 네 명의 형제가 **불치의** 병으로 죽었습니다. 그는 학대를 당했습니다.

Ⅳ Story Writing Paragraph 2

1 Vocabulary

단 어	뜻	단 어	뜻	
fate	운명	accepted	받아들였다	accept의 과거형
unfortunate	불행한, 운이 나쁜	constant	끊임없이 계속되는	
difficult life	힘든 삶	disturbed	방해했다	disturb의 과거형
spiritual	정신적인	lost	잃어버렸다	lose의 과거형
natural talent	천부적 재능, 타고난 재능	painful	고통스러운	
severe	심한	harassed	괴롭혔다	harass의 과거형
mental troubles	정신병			

2 Sentence Writing [형용사의 한정적용법]

1 이 소년은 그의 **불행한** 운명을 받아들였습니다.

2 그의 **힘든** 삶은 어두웠지만, 그는 음악을 좋아했습니다.

3 음악이 그의 **정신적인** 부모가 되었습니다.

4 그는 **천부적** 재능을 가지고 있었습니다.

5 그의 운명은 그를 괴롭혔습니다.

6 그는 **심한** 정신병에 걸렸습니다.

7 그 **끊임없이 계속되는** 병은 그의 일을 방해했습니다.

8 그는 헛소리를 들었습니다.

9 그는 청력을 잃어버렸습니다.

10 그이 **고통스러운** 두통과 복통은 30년간 그를 괴롭혔습니다.

3 Paragraph Writing

이 소년은 그의 **불행한** 운명을 받아들였습니다. 그의 **힘든** 삶은 어두웠지만, 그는 음악을 좋아했습니다. 음악이 그의 **정신적인** 부모가 되었습니다. 그는 **천부적** 재능을 가지고 있었습니다. 그의 운명은 그를 괴롭혔습니다. 그는 **심한** 정신병에 걸렸습니다. 그 **끊임없이 계속되는** 병은 그의 일을 방해했습니다. 그는 헛소리를 들었습니다. 그는 청력을 잃어버렸습니다. 그의 **고통스러운** 두통과 복통은 30년간 그를 괴롭혔습니다.

V Story Writing — Paragraph 3

1 Vocabulary

단어	뜻	단어	뜻
all	모든	dramatic	극적인
a piece of	~의 한 곡, ~의 한 조각	sublime	장엄한
powerful	힘이 넘치는, 강력한	symphony	교향곡
breathtaking	숨막히는	great	위대한
only	단, 단지, 오직	true value	참된 가치, 진정한 가치
sensational	세상을 놀라게 하는		

2 Sentence Writing [형용사의 한정적용법]

1   그는 음악을 사랑했습니다.

2   그는 **모든** 사람들을 사랑했습니다.

3   그는 **힘이 넘치는** 곡을 하나 썼습니다.

4   그 곡은 5년이나 걸렸지만, 그것은 짧았습니다.

5   그 **숨막히는** 곡은 길이가 단지 30분이었습니다.

6   우리는 **세상을 놀라게 한** 이 곡을 매일 듣습니다.

7   그것은 베토벤 5번 교향곡입니다.

8   베토벤은 **비극적인** 삶을 가지고 있었지만, 그는 그의 운명을 극복했습니다.

9   그는 한 **장엄한** 교향곡을 남겼습니다.

10 그 **위대한** 교향곡은 삶의 **참된** 가치를 가르쳐줍니다.

3 Paragraph Writing

> 그는 음악을 사랑했습니다. 그는 **모든** 사람들을 사랑했습니다. 그는 **힘이 넘치는** 곡을 하나 썼습니다. 그 곡은 5년이나 걸렸지만, 그 곡은 짧았습니다. 그 **숨막히는** 곡은 단 30분짜리였습니다. 우리는 **세상을 놀라게 한** 이 곡을 매일 듣습니다. 그것은 베토벤 5번 교향곡입니다. 베토벤은 **비극적인** 삶을 가지고 있었지만, 그는 그의 운명을 극복했습니다. 그는 하나의 **장엄한** 교향곡을 남겼고, 그 **위대한** 교향곡은 삶의 **참된** 가치를 가르쳐줍니다.

VI Error Analysis

This story contains 30 errors. Find and correct them.

His abusive father was ~~alcoholic~~. His mother was a serious tuberculosis
an alcoholic
patients. He had seven brother. His oldest brother was borned blind. His second oldest brother was a mental disability. He's younger brothers was deaf and fatal tuberculosis patients. Four brothers killed of curable diseases. He was abusive.

This boy accepted his unfortunately fate. His difficult life was dark, and he liked music. Music becames his spiritually parents. He had nature talent. His fate tortured him. He has severe mental troubles. The consonant illness disturbed his work. He heard strange things. He lost his hear. His a painful headache and an abdominal pain harassed him during 30 years.

He loved a music. He loved all people. He wrote a peace of powerful music. The music taken five years, but he was short. The breathtaking music was only 30 minutes longer. We listen to this piece of sensational music every day. It is Beethoven's 5th symphony. Beethoven had tragic life, but he overcomes his fate. He left one sublime symphony. This great symphony teaches the true value at life.

3 현재분사 vs 과거분사

I Grammar

1 단어의 형태로 구별할 수 있는 분사(Participle)

① 동사 뒤에 **~ing** 또는 **~ed**가 붙어있으면 **분사**라고 합니다.
② 단어의 뜻은 모르더라도 그 **형태**만 보면 주어진 단어가 분사인지 아닌지는 쉽게 알 수 있습니다.

분사의 형태	동사 + ~ing 또는 동사 + ~ed
분사가 아님	분사라고 할 수 있음
run	runn**ing**
paint	paint**ed**
check and fix	check**ed** and fix**ed**
surprise but smile	surpris**ing** but smil**ing**

2 분사(Participle)의 뜻

① **~ing**로 끝나는 분사 : '**~하는**'의 뜻을 가지고 있습니다.   [능동의 뜻]
② **~ed**로 끝나는 분사 : '**~당한/받은**'의 뜻을 가지고 있습니다.   [수동의 뜻]

~ing	~하는	능동의 뜻
~ed	~당한/받은	수동의 뜻

I like sing**ing** classes.   나는 노래하는 수업을 좋아한다.
I remember the recommend**ed** dates.   나는 추천된 날/추천 받은 날을 기억한다.
This key opens a lock**ed** door.   이 키가 잠긴 문/잠김 당한 문을 연다.

3 분사의 종류

분사는 두 종류가 있습니다.
① ~ing로 끝나는 분사를 **현재분사(Present Participle)**라고 합니다.
② ~ed로 끝나는 분사를 **과거분사(Past Participle)**라고 합니다.

~ing	~하는	현재분사
~ed	~당한/받은	과거분사

[일반동사] investigate 조사하다   The police **investigates** the case.
[현재분사] investigating 조사하는   the **investigating** police
[과거분사] investigated 조사된   the **investigated** case

[일반동사] fix 고치다   This tool **fixes** the door.
[현재분사] fixing 고치는   this **fixing** tool
[과거분사] fixed 고쳐진   the **fixed** door

4 분사(Participle)의 역할

① 분사는 **형용사의 역할**을 합니다. 즉, 명사 앞에 써서 그 명사를 꾸며줍니다.
② 일반 형용사를 쓸 수 있는 모든 자리에 분사 형용사를 쓸 수 있습니다.

현재분사 형용사(Present Participle) + 명사(Noun)
과거분사 형용사(Past Participle) + 명사(Noun)

일반형용사	분사 형용사
a **good** story 좋은 이야기	an **amazing** story 놀라운 이야기
an **urgent** news 급한 뉴스	a **breaking** news 긴급 뉴스
a **sweet** face 귀여운 얼굴	a **smiling** face 웃는 얼굴
a **pretty** room 예쁜 방	a **decorated** room 장식된 방
important names 중요한 이름들	**listed** names 열거된 이름들
wet chairs 젖은 의자들	**painted** chairs 페인트 칠해진 의자들

II. Sentences with Grammar

[분사 형용사]

1. 그 지원자는 **헌신적인/후원적인** 대표자가 되었다.

   ▶ The volunteer became a support____ representative.
   Word Tips Choose the correct one! supporting (　) or supported (　)

2. 그 여자가 그 **엄한** 관리자였다.

   ▶ The woman was the scar____ controller.
   Word Tips Choose the correct one! scaring (　) or scared (　)

3. 그 **선출된** 학생은 영리했다.

   ▶ The select____ student was smart.
   Word Tips Choose the correct one! selecting (　) or selected (　)

4. 그 **기다리는** 손님들은 까다로웠다.

   ▶ The wait____ customers were picky.
   Word Tips Choose the correct one! waiting (　) or waited (　)

5. 모두가 그 **수정된** 제안을 받아들였다.

   ▶ Everybody accepted the revis____ suggestion.
   Word Tips Choose the correct one! revising (　) or revised (　)

6. 그 **초대받은** 사람들은 그 맛을 좋아했다.

   ▶ The invit____ people liked the taste.
   Word Tips Choose the correct one! inviting (　) or invited (　)

7. 그 건물은 **반짝이고 눈부신** 시계를 가지고 있다.

▶ The building has a glitter____ and dazzl____ clock.
Word Tips Choose the correct one!   glittering (   ) or glittered (   ), dazzling (   ) or dazzled (   )

8. 그 **감염된/옮은** 가려움증이 나를 괴롭혔다.

▶ The infect____ itching tortured me.
Word Tips Choose the correct one!   infecting (   ) or infected (   )

9. 그 **계속되는** 잡음이 나의 집중력을 방해했다.

▶ _____
Word Tips Choose the correct one!   continuing (   ) or continued (   )

10. 나의 **박식한** 남동생이 뭔가를 만들었다.

▶ _____
Word Tips Choose the correct one!   educating (   ) or educated (   )

11. 한 **허둥지둥한** 승객이 그의 여권을 잃어버렸다.

▶ _____
Word Tips Choose the correct one!   hurrying (   ) or hurried (   )

12. 그의 **계속되는** 잔소리는 일하는 사람들을 괴롭혔다.

▶ _____
Word Tips Choose the correct one!   nagging (   ) or nagged (   )

13. 그 미술 선생님은 **색종이** 한 장을 준비했다.

▶ _____
Word Tips Choose the correct one!   coloring (   ) or colored (   )

14 그 **터널 뚫는** 공사는 11년이나 걸렸다.

▶ _____
Word Tips Choose the correct one! tunneling (　) or tunneled (　)

15 그의 **감동스런** 연설은 28초였다.

▶ _____
Word Tips Choose the correct one! touching (　) or touched (　)

16 그 참가자들은 **놀라운** 소식을 들었다.

▶ _____
Word Tips Choose the correct one! surprising (　) or surprised (　)

17 그 **장엄한** 경치는 장관이다.

▶ _____
Word Tips Choose the correct one! thrilling (　) or thrilled (　)

18 그 **주목 받는** 도전자는 그의 단점을 극복했다.

▶ _____
Word Tips Choose the correct one! noting (　) or noted (　)

19 그녀의 마지막 말이 **이해할 수 없는** 여운을 남겼다.

▶ _____
Word Tips Choose the correct one! baffling (　) or baffled (　)

20 이 책은 운동의 **변하지 않는** 중요성을 가르친다.

▶ _____
Word Tips Choose the correct one! lasting (　) or lasted (　)

III Story Writing   Paragraph 1

1 Vocabulary

단 어	뜻
abusive	학대하는
untreated	치료를 받지 못한
the oldest brother	첫째 형
suffered blindness	고통을 겪는 장님, 어려움을 겪는 장님
infected	감염된, 옮은, 걸린
spreading diseases	전염병

2 Sentence Writing [분사 형용사]

1 그의 학대하는 아버지는 알코올 중독자였습니다.

2 그의 어머니는 **치료를 받지 못한** 폐결핵 환자였습니다.

3 그는 일곱 명의 형제들이 있었습니다.

4 그의 첫째 형은 **어려움을 겪는** 장님이었습니다.

5 그의 둘째 형은 정신적인 장애를 가지고 있었습니다.

6 그의 동생들은 귀머거리와 폐결핵에 **걸린** 환자였습니다.

7 네 명의 형제가 **전염**병으로 죽었습니다.

8 그는 **학대를 당했**습니다.

3 Paragraph Writing

> 그의 학대하는 아버지는 알코올 중독자였습니다. 그의 어머니는 **치료를 받지 못한** 폐결핵 환자였습니다. 그는 일곱 명의 형제들이 있었습니다. 그의 첫째 형은 **어려움을 겪는** 장님이었습니다. 그의 둘째 형은 정신적인 장애를 가지고 있었습니다. 그의 동생들은 귀머거리와 폐결핵에 **걸린** 환자였습니다. 네 명의 형제가 **전염**병으로 죽었습니다. 그는 **학대를 당했**습니다.

IV Story Writing Paragraph 2

1 Vocabulary

단 어	뜻	단 어	뜻
saddened	슬픈, 불운한	tortured	괴롭혔다
troubled	힘겨운, 괴로운	distressing	괴로움을 주는
supporting	헌신적인, 도와주는	mental troubles	정신병
blessed	축복 받은	continuing	계속되는

2 Sentence Writing [분사 형용사]

1 이 소년은 그의 **슬픈** 운명을 받아들였습니다.

2 그의 **힘겨운** 삶은 어두웠지만, 그는 음악을 좋아했습니다.

3 음악이 그의 **헌신적인** 부모가 되었습니다.

4 그는 **축복받은** 재능을 가지고 있었습니다.

5 그의 운명은 그를 괴롭혔습니다.

6 그는 **괴로움을 주는** 정신병에 걸렸습니다.

7 그 **계속되는** 병은 그의 일을 방해했습니다.

8 그는 헛소리를 들었습니다.

9 그는 청력을 잃어버렸습니다.

10 그의 두통과 복통은 30년간 그를 괴롭혔습니다.

3 Paragraph Writing

이 소년은 그의 **슬픈** 운명을 받아들였습니다. 그의 **힘겨운** 삶은 어두웠지만, 그는 음악을 좋아했습니다. 음악이 그의 **헌신적인** 부모가 되었습니다. 그는 **축복받은** 재능을 가지고 있었습니다. 그의 운명은 그를 괴롭혔습니다. 그는 **괴로움을 주는** 정신병에 걸렸습니다. 그 **계속되는** 병은 그의 일을 방해했습니다. 그는 헛소리를 들었습니다. 그는 청력을 잃어버렸습니다. 그의 두통과 복통은 30년간 그를 괴롭혔습니다.

V Story Writing   Paragraph 3

1 Vocabulary

단어	뜻	단어	뜻
astonishing	놀랄만한	thrilling	장렬한, 스릴 넘치는
amazing music	굉장한 곡, 굉장한 음악	dignified	위엄 있는
celebrated	유명해진, 유명한	lasting value	변하지 않는 가치

2 Sentence Writing [분사 형용사]

1 그는 음악을 사랑했습니다.

2 그는 사람들을 사랑했습니다.

3 그는 **놀랄만한** 곡을 하나 썼습니다.

4 그 곡은 5년이나 걸렸지만, 그것은 짧았습니다.

5 그 **굉장한** 곡은 길이가 단지 30분이었습니다.

6 우리는 이 **유명한** 곡을 매일 듣습니다.

7 그것은 베토벤 5번 교향곡입니다.

8 베토벤은 비극적인 삶을 가지고 있었지만, 그는 그의 운명을 극복했습니다.

9 그는 하나의 **장렬한** 교향곡을 남겼습니다.

10 그 **위엄 있는** 교향곡은 삶의 **변하지 않는** 가치를 가르쳐줍니다.

3 Paragraph Writing

> 그는 음악을 사랑했습니다. 그는 사람들을 사랑했습니다. 그는 **놀랄만한** 곡을 하나 썼습니다. 그 곡은 5년이나 걸렸지만, 그 곡은 짧았습니다. 그 **굉장한** 곡은 길이가 단지 30분이었습니다. 우리는 이 **유명한** 곡을 매일 듣습니다. 그것은 베토벤 5번 교향곡입니다. 베토벤은 비극적인 삶을 가지고 있었지만, 그는 그의 운명을 극복했습니다. 그는 하나의 **장렬한** 교향곡을 남겼고, 그 **위엄 있는** 교향곡은 삶의 **변하지 않는** 가치를 가르쳐줍니다.

VI Error Analysis

This story contains 30 errors. Find and correct them.

His abusive father was an alcoholic. His mother was an ~~intreated~~ *untreated* tuberculosis patient. He has seven brothers. His oldest brother was suffered blindness. His second oldest brothers had a mantel disability. His younger brothers was deaf and effected tuberculosis patients. Four brothers die of spreading diseases. He was abused.

This boy accepted his saddened fate. His traveled life was darks, but he liked musics. Music becam his supporting parents. He had blessed talent. His fate tutored him. He had distressing mental troubles. The counting illness disturb his work. He heard strange things. He losts his hearing. His headaches and abdominal pain harassed him per 30 years.

He loved a music. He loved people. He wrotes a piece of an astonishing music. The music took five ears, but it was shorts. The amazing music was only 30 minutes log. We listen this piece over celebrated music every day. It is beethoven's 5th Symphony. Beethoven had an tragic life, but she overcame his fate. He left one drilling symphony. The symphony dignified teaches the lasting value of life.

4 전치사구의 형용사적 용법

I Grammar

1 전치사구란?

① 전치사 뒤에 명사를 쓴 것을 **전치사구**라고 합니다.
② 전치사 뒤에 사용된 명사를 다른 말로 **전치사의 목적어**라고 하기도 합니다.

| 전치사구 (Prepositional Phrase) | = | 전치사 (Preposition) | + | 명사 (Noun) |

전치사	+ 명사	= 전치사구
in	+ the sea	= **in the sea** 바닷속에
at	+ 12a.m.	= **at 12a.m.** 12시에
for	+ you and me	= **for you and me** 너와 나를 위해서
around	+ the bus station	= **around the bus station** 버스 정류장 주변에

2 전치사구의 형용사적 용법

전치사구가 **주어 뒤**에 쓰여서 주어에 대한 더 많은 정보를 줄 때가 있습니다. 형용사처럼 주어를 내용상 꾸며주고 수식한다고 해서 전치사구의 **형용사적 용법**이라고 합니다.

| 전치사구의 형용사적 용법 | 주어(S) + 전치사구(Prep. Phrase) |

Creatures are mysterious. 생명체들은 신비롭다.
Creatures **in the water** are mysterious. 바닷속에 있는 생명체들은 신비롭다.

A chance is coming. 기회가 오고 있다.
A chance **for you and me** is coming. 너와 나를 위한 기회가 오고 있다.

3 전치사구의 역할

전치사구는 주어를 수식한다는 문법적인 역할 말고도 다음의 세가지 혜택을 우리에게 줍니다.

① 글의 길이를 길게 합니다.
② 글의 내용을 풍부하게 합니다.
③ 글의 길이가 길어지고 내용이 풍부해지므로 전체적인 글의 level이 올라갑니다.

전치사구를 쓰기 전의 낮은 level	→	전치사구를 쓴 후의 높은 level
The movie was interesting.	→	The movie **about the hidden treasure** was interesting.
The stars twinkle.	→	The stars **in the dark sky** twinkle.

4 전치사구를 만들기 위해서 알고 있어야 하는 전치사

다음은 영어 전반에 걸쳐서 많이 사용되는 전치사들이기 때문에 무조건 외우고 있어야 합니다. 전치사의 뜻을 적어 보면서 차근차근 외워 보도록 하세요.

about	_____	inside	_____
above	_____	into	_____
across	_____	like	_____
after	_____	near	_____
against	_____	nearby	_____
along	_____	next	_____
among	_____	of	_____
around	_____	off	_____
as	_____	on	_____
at	_____	outside	_____
before	_____	over	_____
behind	_____	since	_____
below	_____	through	_____
beneath	_____	throughout	_____
beside	_____	till	_____
between	_____	to	_____
beyond	_____	toward	_____
by	_____	under	_____
despite	_____	until	_____
down	_____	upon	_____
during	_____	via	_____
except	_____	with	_____
for	_____	within	_____
from	_____	without	_____
in	_____	worth	_____

II. Sentences with Grammar

[전치사구의 형용사적 용법]

1. **사무실에 있는** 그 여자가 그 엄한 관리자였다.
   ▶ _____
   Word Tips in, scaring

2. **투표를 통해서** 선출된 그 학생은 영리했다.
   ▶ _____
   Word Tips through, vote

3. **줄을 서서** 그 기다리는 손님들은 까다로웠다.
   ▶ _____
   Word Tips in, picky

4. **핵심회원으로써** 모두가 그 수정된 제안을 받아들였다.
   ▶ _____
   Word Tips as, core, members, revised

5. 그 **저녁파티에** 초대받은 사람들은 그 맛을 좋아했다.
   ▶ _____
   Word Tips to, dinner party

6. **길 건너 있는** 그 건물은 반짝이고 눈부신 시계를 가지고 있다.
   ▶ _____
   Word Tips across, glittering, dazzling

54

7 내 피부 위에 옮은/감염된 그 가려움증이 나를 괴롭혔다.

▶ _____
Word Tips on, tortured

8 집밖에서 끊임없이 계속되는 잡음이 나의 집중력을 방해했다.

▶ _____
Word Tips continuing, outside, disturbed

9 나와 함께 있는 나의 박식한 남동생이 뭔가를 만들었다.

▶ _____
Word Tips educated, with

10 공항에 있던 한 허둥지둥 거리던 승객이 그의 여권을 잃어버렸다.

▶ _____
Word Tips in, airport, lost

11 아무것도 아닌 일에 대한 그의 계속되는 잔소리는 일하는 사람들을 괴롭혔다.

▶ _____
Word Tips nagging, over, nothing, harassed

12 학교에 있는 그 미술 선생님은 색종이 한 장을 준비했다.

▶ _____
Word Tips at, school, a piece of

13 강을 따라가는 그 터널 뚫는 공사는 11년이나 걸렸다.

▶ _____
Word Tips tunneling, along, took

14 **개막식전** 그의 감동스런 연설은 단 28초였다.

▶ _____

Word Tips before, opening ceremony

15 **그 회의의** 참가자들은 놀라운 소식을 들었다.

▶ _____

Word Tips in, conference

16 **산 너머** 장엄한 경치는 장관이다.

▶ _____

Word Tips thrilling, over, mountain, sublime

17 **그 경기에 참가한** 그 주목 받는 도전자는 그의 단점을 극복했다.

▶ _____

Word Tips in, competition, overcame

18 **평화에 관한** 그녀의 마지막 말이 이해할 수 없는 여운을 남겼다.

▶ _____

Word Tips about, peace, suggestiveness

19 **올해의** 책은 운동의 변하지 않는 중요성을 가르친다.

▶ _____

Word Tips of, the year, exercise

III. Story Writing Paragraph 1

1 Vocabulary

단 어	뜻	단 어	뜻
at	~(장소)에 있는	genetic disease	선천적 병
in	~(장소)안에 있는	in the family	가족 가운데
in the bed	침대에 누워있는	infected	감염된, 옮은, 걸린
untreated	치료 받지 못한	among	~(셋 이상) 가운데
with	~와 함께, ~을 가지고		

2 Sentence Writing [전치사구의 형용사적 용법]

1. **집에 있는** 그의 아버지는 알코올 중독자였습니다.

2. **침대에 누워있는** 그의 어머니는 치료 받지 못한 폐결핵 환자였습니다.

3. 그는 일곱 명의 형제들이 있었습니다.

4. **유전병을 가지고 있는** 그의 첫째 형은 고통받는 장님이었습니다.

5. **가족 가운데** 그의 둘째 형은 정신적인 장애를 가지고 있었습니다.

6. **집안에 있는** 그의 동생들은 귀머거리와 폐결핵에 걸린 환자였습니다.

7. **그들 가운데** 네 명의 형제가 전염병으로 죽었습니다.

8. 그는 학대를 당했습니다.

3 Paragraph Writing

집에 있는 그의 아버지는 알코올 중독자였습니다. **침대에 누워있는** 그의 어머니는 치료 받지 못한 폐결핵 환자였습니다. 그는 일곱 명의 형제들이 있었습니다. **유전병을 가지고 있는** 그의 첫째 형은 고통받는 장님이었습니다. **가족 가운데** 그의 둘째 형은 정신적인 장애를 가지고 있었습니다. **집안에 있는** 그의 동생들은 귀머거리와 폐결핵에 걸린 환자였습니다. **그들 가운데** 네 명의 형제가 전염병으로 죽었습니다. 그는 학대를 당했습니다.

IV Story Writing — Paragraph 2

1 Vocabulary

단어	뜻	단어	뜻
under	~아래에, ~아래에서, ~아래로	supporting	헌신적인, 도와주는
unfortunate	불행한	as	~로서 (자격, 신분, 지위)
environment	환경	musician	음악가
around	~주변에	distressing	괴로움을 주는
about	~에 관하여	continuing	계속되는
hope	희망	during	~하는 동안에

2 Sentence Writing [전치사구의 형용사적 용법]

1 **불행한 환경 아래 있는** 이 소년은 그의 슬픈 운명을 받아들였습니다.

2 **그의 주변에 있는** 그의 힘겨운 삶은 어두웠지만, 그는 음악을 좋아했습니다.

3 **사랑과 희망에 대한** 음악이 그의 헌신적인 부모가 되었습니다.

4 그는 축복받은 재능을 가지고 있었습니다.

5 **음악가로서의** 그의 운명은 그를 괴롭혔습니다.

6 그는 괴로움을 주는 정신병에 걸렸습니다.

7 **그의 몸 속에서** 계속되는 그 병은 그의 일을 방해했습니다.

8 그는 헛소리를 들었습니다.

9 그는 청력을 잃어버렸습니다.

10 **그가 일하는 동안** 그의 두통과 복통은 30년간 그를 괴롭혔습니다.

3 Paragraph Writing

> **불행한 환경 아래 있는** 이 소년은 그의 슬픈 운명을 받아들였습니다. **그의 주변에 있는** 그의 힘겨운 삶은 어두웠지만, 그는 음악을 좋아했습니다. **사랑과 희망에 대한** 음악이 그의 헌신적인 부모가 되었습니다. 그는 축복받은 재능을 가지고 있었습니다. **음악가로서의** 그의 운명은 그를 괴롭혔습니다. 그는 괴로움을 주는 정신병에 걸렸습니다. **그의 몸 속에서** 계속되는 그 병은 그의 일을 방해했습니다. 그는 헛소리를 들었습니다. 그는 청력을 잃어버렸습니다. **그가 일하는 동안** 그의 두통과 복통은 30년간 그를 괴롭혔습니다.

V Story Writing — Paragraph 3

1 Vocabulary

단 어	뜻	단 어	뜻
for	~동안	thrilling	장렬한, 스릴 넘치는
amazing	놀랄만한	from	~로부터
celebrated	유명한, 알려진	passion	열정
musical talent	음악적 소질	lasting	영구적인

2 Sentence Writing [전치사구의 형용사적 용법]

1. 그는 음악을 사랑했습니다. 그는 사람들을 사랑했습니다.

2. 그는 **오케스트라를 위해서** 놀랄만한 곡을 하나 썼습니다.

3. 그 곡은 5년이나 걸렸지만, 그것은 짧았습니다.

4. 그 굉장한 곡은 길이가 단지 30분이었습니다.

5. 우리는 이 유명한 곡을 매일 듣습니다.

6. 그것은 베토벤 5번 교향곡입니다.

7. **음악적 소질을 지닌** 베토벤은 비극적인 삶을 가지고 있었습니다.

8. 그는 그의 운명을 극복했습니다.

9. 그는 하나의 장렬한 교향곡을 남겼습니다.

10. **그의 열정으로부터 나온** 그 위엄 있는 교향곡은 삶의 영구적인 가치를 가르쳐줍니다.

3 Paragraph Writing

그는 음악을 사랑했습니다. 그는 사람들을 사랑했습니다. 그는 **오케스트라를 위해서** 놀랄만한 곡을 하나 썼습니다. 그 곡은 5년이나 걸렸지만, 그것은 짧았습니다. 그 굉장한 곡은 길이가 단지 30분이었습니다. 우리는 이 유명한 곡을 매일 듣습니다. 그것은 베토벤 5번 교향곡입니다. **음악적 소질을 지닌** 베토벤은 비극적인 삶을 가지고 있었습니다, 그러나 그는 그의 운명을 극복했습니다. 그는 하나의 장렬한 교향곡을 남겼습니다. **그의 열정으로부터 나온** 그 위엄 있는 교향곡은 삶의 영구적인 가치를 가르쳐줍니다.

VI Error Analysis

This story contains 35 errors. Find and correct them.

His father at home was an alcoholic. His mother ~~in bed~~ *in the bed* was untreated tuberculosis patient. She had seven brothers. His oldest brother for a genetic disease was suffered blindness. His second oldest brother in the family head a mental disability. His younger brothers side the house were deaf and infected tuberculosis patient. Four brother among their died of spreading diseases. He was abusing.

This boy under the fortunate environment accepted his saddened fate. He's troubled life round him were dark, but he liked music. A music above love and hope became his supported parents. He had blessed talent. His fate as musician tortured himself. He had distressing mental troubles. The continued illness in his body disturbed his walk. He heard strange thinks. He lost his hearing. His headache and abdominal pain during his work harassed him for 30 years.

He love music. He loved people. He writted a piece of an astonishing music for an orchestra. The music took five years, but it was shutter. The amazing music was only 30 minuets long. We listen to this piece of celebrated music every day. It was Beethovens 5th Symphony. Beethoven beyond musical talent had a tragic life, but he over came his fate. He lefted one thrilling symphony. The dignifying symphony about his passion teaches the lasted value of life.

5 합성전치사

I Grammar

1 합성전치사란?

① **여러 개의 단어**가 모여서 전치사가 된 것을 말합니다.
② 상급의 실력을 가지기 위해서 꼭 알고 있어야 합니다.

> **합성전치사(Complex Preposition) + 명사(Noun)**

[2개의 단어로 이루어진 전치사] along + with = along with
along with us 우리와 함께

[3개의 단어로 이루어진 전치사] on + behalf + of = on behalf of
on behalf of the management 경영진을 대신하여

[4개의 단어로 이루어진 전치사] in + the + course + of = in the course of
in the course of the test 그 시험 동안에

2 [합성전치사 + 명사]의 위치

[합성전치사 + 명사]는 주로 **문장 뒤**에 놓입니다. 단, 강조를 목적으로 할 때는 문장 앞에 쓸 수 있습니다.

> **문장(Sentence) + 합성전치사(Complex Preposition) + 명사(Noun)**

합성전치사 사용 전	→	[합성전치사 + 명사]를 문장 뒤에 쓴 것
He designed it. 그는 그것을 디자인했다.	→	He designed it **along with** a new style. 그는 그것을 새로운 스타일과 함께 디자인했다.
I came. 나는 왔다.	→	I came **on behalf of** the management. 나는 경영진을 대신해서 왔다.
Everybody was quiet. 모두가 조용했다.	→	Everybody was quiet **in the course of** the test. 모두는 시험 보는 동안에 조용했다.

3 합성전치사의 효과

글의 **level**을 높이는데 중요한 역할을 합니다.

[일반전치사 사용] We eat regularly **for** our health.
우리는 우리의 건강을 위해서 규칙적으로 식사를 합니다.

[합성전치사 사용] We eat regularly **for the sake of** our health.
우리는 우리의 건강을 목적으로 규칙적으로 식사를 합니다.

[일반전치사 사용] People made a reservation **before** the holiday.
사람들은 휴가 전에 예약을 했다.

[합성전치사 사용] People made a reservation **at the beginning of** the holiday.
사람들은 휴가 시작 때에 예약을 했다.

4 합성전치사의 종류

across from	~의 맞은편에	in favor of	~에 찬성하여
alongside of	along with보다 강조의 의미	in keeping with	~와 일치해서, ~와 어울려서
along with	~와 함께	in lieu of	~의 대신으로
as a result of	~의 결과로써	in regard to	~에 관해서
as well as	~뿐만 아니라 ~도	in response to	~에 응하여, ~에 답하여
at the beginning of	~의 시작 때에	in return for	~에 대한 답례로
away from	~로부터 떠나서, ~벗어나서	in spite of	~에도 불구하고
because of	~때문에	in terms of	~의 점에서 보면
by means of	~의 수단으로	in the course of	~의 동안에
by way of	~에 경유하여, ~을 지나서	instead of	~대신에
close to	~에 근접한, ~에 가까운	next to	~옆에
due to	~때문에	on account of	~이기 때문에, ~이므로
except for	~을 제외하면	on behalf of	~대신에, 대표하여
for the sake of	~을 위해서, ~을 목적으로	on pain of	~에 대한 대가로
in accordance with	~에 일치하여	on the part of	~의 부분으로써
in addition to	~에 더하여	on top of	~보다 우위에 서서
in case of	~의 경우를 대비해서	out of	~안에서 밖으로, ~안으로부터
in charge of	~에 책임이 있는	rather than	~하기 보다는 차라리
in common with	~와 같은, ~와 공통인	such as	~와 같은, 예를 들어서
in connection with	~와 연관이 있는, ~와 연결된	together with	~와 더불어서
in comparison with	~와 비교하여 보면	up to	~까지, ~에 이르기 까지
in contrast to	~와는 대조적으로	with respect to	~에 관하여
in contrast with	~와는 현저히 다른		

II. Sentences with Grammar

[합성전치사의 사용]

1. 그 지원자는 회의 **하는 동안에** 후원적인 대표자가 되었다.

   ▶ _____

   Word Tips in the course of, meeting

2. 투표를 통해서 선출된 그 학생은 교실 관리**부분에서 볼 때** 영리했다.

   ▶ _____

   Word Tips on the part of, class management

3. 그 손님들은 다른 사람들**과 비교해 볼 때** 까다로웠다.

   ▶ _____

   Word Tips in comparison with, others

4. 모두가 그 수정된 제안을 그것의 간편성 **때문에** 받아들였다.

   ▶ _____

   Word Tips because of, its, simplicity

5. 그 저녁파티에 초대 받은 사람들은 그 달콤한 향기**에 더해서** 그 맛을 좋아했다.

   ▶ _____

   Word Tips in addition to, sweet smell

6 길 건너 있는 그 건물은 반짝이고 눈부신 시계를 그 지붕 **위에** 가지고 있다.

▶ _____

Word Tips on top of, roof

7 내 피부에 옮은/감염된 그 가려움증은 진물**과 함께** 나를 괴롭혔다.

▶ _____

Word Tips together with, ooze

8 그 끊임없이 계속되는 잡음은 나의 잠**뿐만 아니라** 나의 집중력**도** 방해했다.

▶ _____

Word Tips as well as, sleep

9 나의 남동생이 그것**으로부터** 무엇인가를 만들었다.

▶ _____

Word Tips out of

10 공항에 있던 한 승객이 그의 서류 가방**과 함께** 그의 여권을 잃어버렸다.

▶ _____

Word Tips along with, briefcase

11 그의 계속되는 잔소리는 그 사람 **옆에서** 일하는 사람들을 괴롭혔다.

▶ _____

Word Tips next to

67

12 그 미술 선생님은 빈 종이**대신에** 색종이 한 장을 준비했다.

▶ _____

Word Tips instead of, plain paper

13 그 터널 뚫는 공사는 그것의 어려움 **때문에** 11년이나 걸렸다.

▶ _____

Word Tips because of, difficulties

14 그 회의의 참가자들은 일정**에 관해서** 놀라운 소식을 들었다.

▶ _____

Word Tips in regard to, schedule

15 그 장엄한 경치는 나쁜 날씨**에도 불구하고** 장관이다.

▶ _____

Word Tips in spite of, bad, weather

16 그 경기에 참가한 그 도전자는 포기**하는 대신에** 그의 단점을 극복했다.

▶ _____

Word Tips instead of, giving up

17 평화에 관한 그녀의 마지막 말이 하나의 질문**과 함께** 이해할 수 없는 여운을 남겼다.

▶ _____

Word Tips alongside of, question

III. Story Writing   Paragraph 1

1 Vocabulary

단 어	뜻	단 어	뜻
as a result of	~의 결과로	brain tumor	뇌종양
heavy drinking	폭주	among	~(셋 이상) 가운데
genetic disease	선천적 병	died of	~으로 죽었다
because of	~때문에	in connection with	~와 연결되어서, ~와 관련된

2 Sentence Writing   [합성전치사의 사용]

1 집에 있는 그의 아버지는 **폭주로 인한 결과로** 알코올 중독자였습니다.

2 침대에 누워있는 그의 어머니는 치료 받지 못한 폐결핵 환자였습니다.

3 그는 일곱 명의 형제들이 있었습니다.

4 유전병을 가지고 있는 그의 첫째 형은 만성 장님이었습니다.

5 가족 가운데 그의 둘째 형은 **뇌종양 때문에** 정신적인 장애를 가지고 있었습니다.

6 집안에 있는 그의 동생들은 귀머거리와 폐결핵에 걸린 환자였습니다.

7 그들 가운데 네 명의 형제가 **독감과 관련된** 전염병으로 죽었습니다.

8 그는 학대를 당했습니다.

3 Paragraph Writing

집에 있는 그의 아버지는 **폭주로 인한 결과로** 알코올 중독자였습니다. 침대에 누워있는 그의 어머니는 치료 받지 못한 폐결핵 환자였습니다. 그는 일곱 명의 형제들이 있었습니다. 유전병을 가지고 있는 그의 첫째 형은 만성 장님이었습니다. 가족 가운데 그의 둘째 형은 **뇌종양 때문에** 정신적인 장애를 가지고 있었습니다. 집안에 있는 그의 남동생들은 귀머거리와 폐결핵에 걸린 환자였습니다. 그들 가운데 네 명의 형제가 **독감과 관련된** 전염병으로 죽었습니다. 그는 학대를 당했습니다.

Ⅳ Story Writing Paragraph 2

1 Vocabulary

단 어	뜻
flu	독감
as	~로서 (자격, 신분, 지위)
life	일생
illness	질병
emotion	감정
such as	~와 같은, 예를 들어서
knocking	두드리는 것
scratching	긁는 것
crying	우는 것
unfortunate environment	불행한 환경
instead of	~대신에
giving up	포기하는 것
A as well as B	B뿐만 아니라 A도
in contrast to	~와 대조적으로
mental troubles	정신병
tragic life	비극적인 삶
in the course of	~동안에
due to	~때문에
in addition to	~에 더하여

2 Sentence Writing [부사절의 사용]

1. 불행한 환경 아래 있는 이 소년은 **포기하는 대신에** 그의 슬픈 운명을 받아들였습니다.

2. 그의 주변에 있는 그의 힘겨운 삶은 어두웠지만, 그는 음악을 좋아했습니다.

3. 사랑과 희망에 대한 음악이 **친구뿐만 아니라** 그의 헌신적인 부모**도** 되었습니다.

4   그는 **그의 비극적인 삶과는 대조적으로** 축복받은 재능을 가지고 있었습니다.
_____
_____

5   음악가로서의 그의 운명은 **그의 일생 동안** 그를 괴롭혔습니다.
_____
_____

6   그는 **병 때문에** 정신병에 걸렸습니다.
_____
_____

7   그의 몸 속에 계속되는 그 병은 **그의 감정뿐만 아니라** 그의 일**도** 방해했습니다.
_____
_____

8   그는 **두드리고, 긁고, 그리고 우는 것과 같은** 헛소리를 들었습니다.
_____
_____

9   그는 **이 병 때문에** 청력을 잃어버렸습니다.
_____
_____

10 그가 일하는 동안 그의 두통과 복통은 **그의 정신병에 더하여** 30년간 그를 괴롭혔습니다.
_____
_____
_____

3 Paragraph Writing

불행한 환경아래 있는 이 소년은 **포기하는 대신에** 그의 슬픈 운명을 받아들였습니다. 그의 주변에 있는 그의 삶은 힘겨웠지만, 그는 음악을 좋아했습니다. 사랑과 희망에 대한 음악이 **친구뿐만 아니라** 그의 헌신적인 부모**도** 되었습니다. 그는 **그의 비극적인 삶과는 대조적으로** 축복받은 재능을 가지고 있었습니다. 음악가로서 그의 운명은 **그의 일생 동안** 그를 괴롭혔습니다. 그는 **병 때문에** 정신병에 걸렸습니다. 그의 몸 속에 계속되는 그 병은 그의 **감정뿐만 아니라** 그의 일**도** 방해했습니다. 그는 **두드리고, 긁고, 그리고 우는 것과 같은** 헛소리를 들었습니다. 그는 **이 병 때문에** 청력을 잃어버렸습니다. 그가 일하는 동안 그의 두통과 복통은 **그의 정신병에 더하여** 30년간 그를 괴롭혔습니다.

Ⅴ Story Writing   Paragraph 3

1 Vocabulary

단 어	뜻	단 어	뜻
in spite of	~에도 불구하고	in return for	~에 대한 보답으로
suffering	고통	in terms of	~의 면에서 볼 때
passion	열정	playing time	연주시간
patience	인내	together with	~와 더불어

2 Sentence Writing [합성전치사의 사용]

1. 그는 **이런 고통에도 불구하고** 음악을 사랑했습니다.

2. 그는 **이런 아픔에도 불구하고** 사람들을 사랑했습니다.

3. 그는 오케스트라를 위해서 **그의 재능에 대한 보답으로** 놀랄만한 곡을 하나 썼습니다.

4. 사람들을 위한 그 곡은 5년이나 걸렸습니다.

5. 그 곡은 **연주시간의 면에서 볼 때** 짧았습니다.

6. 그 곡은 길이가 단지 30분이었습니다.

7. 우리는 이 유명한 곡을 매일 듣습니다.

8. 그것은 베토벤 5번 교향곡입니다.

9. 음악적 소질을 지닌 베토벤은 비극적인 삶을 가지고 있었습니다.

10. 그는 그의 속에 있었던 그 운명을 극복했습니다. 그는 하나의 장렬한 교향곡을 남겼습니다.

11. 그의 운명으로부터 나온 그 위엄 있는 교향곡은 **그의 열정과 인내와 더불어** 삶의 영구적인 가치를 가르쳐줍니다.

3 Paragraph Writing

그는 **이런 고통에도 불구하고** 음악을 사랑했습니다. 그는 **이런 아픔에도 불구하고** 사람들을 사랑했습니다. 그는 오케스트라를 위해서 **그의 재능에 대한 보답으로** 놀랄만한 곡을 하나 썼습니다. 사람들을 위한 그 곡은 5년이나 걸렸습니다, 하지만 그 곡은 **연주시간의 면에서 볼 때** 짧았습니다. 그 곡은 길이가 단지 30분이었습니다. 우리는 이 유명한 곡을 매일 듣습니다. 그것은 베토벤 5번 교향곡입니다. 음악적 소질을 지닌 베토벤은 비극적인 삶을 가지고 있었지만, 그는 그의 속에 있었던 그 운명을 극복했습니다. 그는 하나의 장렬한 교향곡을 남겼습니다. 그의 운명으로부터 나온 그 위엄 있는 교향곡은 **그의 열정과 인내와 더불어** 삶의 영구적인 가치를 가르쳐줍니다.

VI Error Analysis

This story contains 35 errors. Find and correct them.

His father at a home was an alcoholic as result of heavy drinking. His mother in the bed was an untreating tuberculosis patience. He had seven brothers. His oldest brother with a genetic disease was confirmed blind. His second oldest brother in the family had a mental disability because the brain tumor. His younger brothers inside the house were deaf and infected tuberculosis patients. Four brothers among them dying of the spreading diseases in contact with the flu. He was abused.

This boy under the unfortunate environment accepted his saddened fate instead off giving up. His troubled life among him was dark, but he liked music. Music about love and a hope be came his supporting parents as well as friends. He had blessed talent in contrast for his tragic life. His fate as a magician tortured him in course of his life. He had mental troubles due to illness. The continuing illness in its body disturbed its work as well as his motion. He heard strange things such as knocking, scratching, crying. He lost his hearing because this illness. His head ache and abdominal pain during his work harassed him from 30 years in addition his mental troubles.

He loved music despite of this suffering. He loved people in spite of this pain. He written a piece of astonishing music for an orchestra in return his talent. The music of people took five year, but it was short in terms for the playing time. The music was only 30 minutes long. We listen to this piece of celebrated music every day. It's Beethoven's 5th Symphony. Beethoven for talent musical had a tragic life, but he overcame the fate inside him. He left one thrilling symphony. A dignified symphony form his fate teaches the lasting value of life together over his passion and patient.

6 합성전치사의 강조

I Grammar

1 합성전치사의 강조용법

① 내용상 중요하거나 강조하고 싶은 것은 먼저 쓰거나 말할 수 있습니다.
② 합성전치사는 주로 문장 뒤에 쓰이지만 내용상 먼저 말해서 강조할 필요가 있다고 느낄 때에는 **문장 앞**에 쓸 수 있습니다.

> 합성전치사(Complex Preposition) + 명사(Noun), 문장

[because of의 일반적인 사용] We kept the secret **because of** you.
우리는 비밀을 지켰어 너 때문에.

[because of를 앞에 써서 강조] **Because of** you, we kept the secret.
너 때문에 우리는 비밀을 지켰다.

[in spite of의 일반적인 사용] We went out **in spite of** the bad weather.
우리는 나갔다 나쁜 날씨에도 불구하고.

[in spite of를 앞에 써서 강조] **In spite of** the bad weather, we went out.
나쁜 날씨에도 불구하고 우리는 나갔다.

2 문장 앞으로 보내지 않는 합성전치사

① 대부분의 합성전치사는 강조를 목적으로 할 때 문장 앞으로 보낼 수 있습니다.
② 하지만, **as well as**와 **such as**는 강조의 용도로 사용하지 않습니다.

[자연스러운 문장] The program was informative **as well as** interesting.
그 프로그램은 재미있을 뿐만 아니라 내용면에서도 좋았다.

[부자연스러운 문장] **As well as** interesting, the program was informative.

[자연스러운 문장] He likes activities **such as** jogging, swimming, and hiking.
그는 조깅, 수영, 그리고 등산과 같은 활동을 좋아한다.

[부자연스러운 문장] **Such as** jogging, swimming, and hiking, he likes activities.

3 합성전치사와 일반전치사를 동시에 사용

한 문장 안에 합성전치사와 일반 전치사를 모두 사용하면 문장이 길어지고 자세해집니다.

① He asked a few questions **about** the meaning **of** life.
그는 삶의 의미에 대해서 몇 가지 질문을 했다.

He asked a few questions **at the beginning of** the seminar.
그는 세미나를 시작할 때 몇 가지 질문을 했다.

He asked a few questions **about** the meaning **of** life **at the beginning of** the seminar.
그는 세미나를 시작할 때 삶의 의미에 대해서 몇 가지 질문을 했다.

② We showed a video clip **to** the students.
우리는 학생들에게 동영상을 보여주었다.

We showed a video clip **in the course of** the presentation.
우리는 발표하는 동안에 동영상을 보여주었다.

We showed a video clip **to** the students **in the course of** the presentation.
우리는 발표하는 동안에 학생들에게 동영상을 보여주었다.

Ⅱ Sentences with Grammar

[합성전치사의 강조]

1. 교실 관리**부분에서 볼 때** 투표를 통해서 선출된 그 학생은 영리했다.

   ▶ _____

   Word Tips on the part of, class management, through, vote

2. 다른 사람**과 비교해 볼 때** 그 손님들은 까다로웠다.

   ▶ _____

   Word Tips in comparison with, others

3. 그것의 간편성 **때문에** 모두가 그 수정된 제안을 받아들였다.

   ▶ _____

   Word Tips because of, simplicity, revised

4. 회의 **하는 동안에** 그 지원자는 후원적인 대표자가 되었다.

   ▶ _____

   Word Tips in the course of, meeting, volunteer, supporting

5. 그 달콤한 향기**에 더해서** 그 저녁파티에 초대 받은 사람들은 그 맛을 좋아했다.

   ▶ _____

   Word Tips in addition to, sweet smell

6 길 건너 있는 그 건물은 그 지붕 **위에** 반짝이고 눈부신 시계를 가지고 있다.

▶ _____

Word Tips on top of, across, glittering, dazzling

7 그의 서류 가방**과 함께** 공항에 있던 한 승객이 그의 여권을 잃어버렸다.

▶ _____

Word Tips along with, lost

8 백지**대신에** 그 미술 선생님은 색종이 한 장을 준비했다.

▶ _____

Word Tips instead of, plain paper, prepared, a piece of, colored

9 그것의 어려움 **때문에** 그 터널 뚫는 공사는 11년이나 걸렸다.

▶ _____

Word Tips because of, tunneling

10 다른 긴 연설**에 비해서** 개막식전 그의 감동스런 연설은 28초였다.

▶ _____

Word Tips in contrast to, other, ceremony

81

11 그 일정**에 관해서** 그 회의의 참가자들은 놀라운 소식을 들었다.

▶ _____

_____

Word Tips in regard to, conference, surprising

12 나쁜 날씨**에도 불구하고** 그 장엄한 경치는 장관이다.

▶ _____

Word Tips in spite of, thrilling, sublime

13 포기**하는 대신에** 그 경기에 참가한 그 도전자는 그의 단점을 극복했다.

▶ _____

Word Tips instead of, giving up, competition, shortcomings

14 하나의 질문**과 함께** 평화에 관한 그녀의 마지막 말이 이해할 수 없는 여운을 남겼다.

▶ _____

_____

Word Tips alongside of, baffling, suggestiveness

III. Story Writing   Paragraph 1

1 Vocabulary

단 어	뜻
as a result of	~의 결과로
because of	~ 때문에
in connection with	~와 연결되어서, ~와 연결된

2 Sentence Writing [합성전치사의 강조]

1. **폭주로 인한 결과로**, 집에 있는 그의 아버지는 알코올 중독자였습니다.

2. 침대에 누워있는 그의 어머니는 치료 받지 못한 폐결핵 환자였습니다.

3. 그는 일곱 명의 형제들이 있었습니다.

4. 유전병을 가지고 있는 그의 첫째 형은 만성 장님이었습니다.

5. **뇌종양 때문에**, 가족 가운데 그의 둘째 형은 정신적 장애를 가지고 있었습니다.

6. 집안에 있는 그의 남동생들은 귀머거리와 폐결핵에 걸린 환자였습니다.

7. **독감과 관련하여**, 그들 가운데 네 명의 형제가 전염병으로 죽었습니다.

8. 그는 학대를 당했습니다.

3 Paragraph Writing

> **폭주로 인한 결과로**, 집에 있는 그의 아버지는 알코올 중독자였습니다. 침대에 누워 있는 그의 어머니는 치료 받지 못한 폐결핵 환자였습니다. 그는 일곱 명의 형제들이 있었습니다. 유전병을 가지고 있는 그의 첫째 형은 만성 장님이었습니다. **뇌종양 때문에**, 가족 가운데 그의 둘째 형은 정신적 장애를 가지고 있었습니다. 집안에 있는 그의 남동생들은 귀머거리와 폐결핵에 걸린 환자였습니다. **독감과 관련하여**, 그들 가운데 네 명의 형제가 전염병으로 죽었습니다. 그는 학대를 당했습니다.

IV Story Writing Paragraph 2

1 Vocabulary

단 어	뜻	단 어	뜻
instead of	~대신에	because of	~ 때문에 (due to보다 정식의 표현)
in contrast to	~와 대조적으로	in addition to	~에 더하여

2 Sentence Writing [합성전치사의 강조]

1 **포기하는 대신에**, 이 소년은 불행한 환경아래 있는 그의 운명을 받아들였습니다.

2 그의 주변에 있는 그의 힘겨운 삶은 어두웠지만, 그는 음악을 좋아했습니다.

3 사랑과 희망에 대한 음악이 **친구뿐만 아니라** 헌신적인 부모**도** 되었습니다.

4 **그의 비극적인 삶과는 대조적으로**, 그는 축복받은 재능을 가지고 있었습니다.

5 **그의 일생 동안**, 음악가로서 그의 운명은 그를 괴롭혔습니다.

6 **그의 병 때문에**, 그는 정신병에 걸렸습니다.

7 그의 몸 속에 계속되는 그 병은 **그의 감정뿐만 아니라** 그의 일**도** 방해했습니다.

8 그는 **두드리고, 긁고, 그리고 우는 것과 같은** 헛소리를 들었습니다.

9 **이 병 때문에**, 그는 청력을 잃어버렸습니다.

10 **그의 정신병에 더하여**, 그가 일하는 동안 그의 두통과 복통은 30년간 그를 괴롭혔습니다.

3 Paragraph Writing

포기하는 대신에, 이 소년은 **불행한 환경아래 있는** 그의 운명을 받아들였습니다. 그의 주변에 있는 그의 힘겨운 삶은 어두웠지만, 그는 음악을 좋아했습니다. 사랑과 희망에 대한 음악이 **친구뿐만 아니라** 헌신적인 부모**도** 되었습니다. **그의 비극적인 삶과는 대조적으로**, 그는 축복받은 재능을 가지고 있었습니다. **그의 일생 동안**, 음악가로서 그의 운명은 그를 괴롭혔습니다. **그의 병 때문에**, 그는 정신병에 걸렸습니다. 그의 몸 속에 계속되는 그 병은 그의 **감정뿐만 아니라** 그의 일**도** 방해했습니다. 그는 **두드리고, 긁고, 그리고 우는 것과 같은** 헛소리를 들었습니다. **이 병 때문에**, 그는 청력을 잃어버렸습니다. **그의 정신병에 더하여**, 그가 일하는 동안 그의 두통과 복통은 30년간 그를 괴롭혔습니다.

V Story Writing Paragraph 3

1 Vocabulary

단 어	뜻	단 어	뜻
in spite of	~에도 불구하고	in terms of	~의 면에서 보면, ~의 각도에서 보면
in return for	~에 대한 화답으로, ~에 대한 보답으로	together with	~와 더불어

2 Sentence Writing [합성전치사의 강조]

1 **이런 고통에도 불구하고**, 그는 음악을 사랑했습니다.

2 **이런 아픔에도 불구하고**, 그는 사람들을 사랑했습니다.

3 **그의 재능에 대한 보답으로**, 그는 오케스트라를 위해서 놀랄만한 곡을 하나 썼습니다.

4 사람들을 위한 그 곡은 5년이나 걸렸습니다, 하지만 **연주시간의 면에서 볼 때**, 그것은 짧았습니다.

5 그 곡은 길이가 단지 30분이었습니다.

6 우리는 이 유명한 곡을 매일 듣습니다.

7 그것은 베토벤 5번 교향곡입니다.

8 **음악적 소실과 함께**, 그는 비극적인 삶을 가지고 있었습니다, 그러나 그는 그의 속에 있었던 그 운명을 극복했습니다.

9 그는 한 장렬한 교향곡을 남겼습니다.

10 **그의 열정과 인내와 더불어**, 그의 운명으로부터 나온 이 위엄 있는 교향곡은 삶의 영구적인 가치를 가르쳐줍니다.

3 Paragraph Writing

이런 고통에도 불구하고, 그는 음악을 사랑했습니다. **이런 아픔에도 불구하고**, 그는 사람들을 사랑했습니다. **그의 재능에 대한 보답으로**, 그는 오케스트라를 위해서 놀랄만한 곡을 하나 썼습니다. 사람들을 위한 그 곡은 5년이나 걸렸습니다, 하지만 **연주시간의 면에서 볼 때**, 그것은 짧았습니다. 그 곡은 길이가 단지 30분이었습니다. 우리는 이 유명한 곡을 매일 듣습니다. 그것은 베토벤 5번 교향곡입니다. **음악적 소실과 함께**, 그는 비극적인 삶을 가지고 있었습니다, 그러나 그는 그의 속에 있었던 그 운명을 극복했습니다. 그는 한 장렬한 교향곡을 남겼습니다. **그의 열정과 인내와 더불어**, 그의 운명으로부터 나온 이 위엄 있는 교향곡은 삶의 영구적인 가치를 가르쳐줍니다.

VI Error Analysis

This story contains 40 errors. Find and correct them.

As the result of heavy drinking, his father at home was an alcoholics. His mother in the bed was an untreated tuberculosis patient. He had sevens brothers. His oldest brother with a genet disease was confirmed blinder. Because the brain tumor, his second oldest brothers in the family had a mental disability. His younger brothers inside the house wore deafs and infected tuberculosis patients. For connection with the flu, four brothers among them died of the spraying diseases. He was abused.

In stead of giving up, this boy accepted his fate under a unfortunate environment. His troubled life around him was dark but, he liked music. Music about loves and hopes became his supporting parentals as will as friends. Incontrast to his tragic life, he had blessed talent. In the courses of his life, his fate as a musician tortured him. Due of the illness, he had mental troubles. The continuing illness in his body disrobed his work well as his emotion. He heard strange things such as knockings, scratching, and crying. Be cause of this illness, he lost his hearing. In addition for his mental troubles, his headache and abdominal pain during work his harassed him for 30 year's.

Inspite of this suffering, he loved music. In spite of this painless, he loved people. In returning for his talent, he wrote a piece of estonishing music for an orchestra. The music for people took five years, but in term of the playtime, it was short. The music was only 30 minutes long. We listen to this piece of celebrated music every day. It is Beethovens' 5th Symphony. Long with magical talent, he had a traffic life, but he is overcame the fate inside him. He left one thrilling symphony. All together with his passion and patience, this dignified symphony from his fate teaches the lasting value of life.

Symphony

앞에 나온 story는 특정한 문법을 공부하기 위한 story였습니다.

문법공부를 위해 만들어진 story는 학습효과의 증대를 위해서 특정 문법을 반복 학습 하도록 유도하다 보니까 내용이 부자연스러워질 수 있습니다.

여기에 소개된 story는 문법보다는 내용이 자연스러워 지도록 Rewriting한 story 입니다.

A boy once grew up in a very sad household. He had a father who was a heavy drinker. Due to his heavy drinking, along with his family problems, he became an alcoholic. His mother would daily lay in bed, suffering from untreated tuberculosis. He had seven brothers, some of whom also had ailments. His oldest brother had a genetic disease that caused him to go blind. His second oldest brother was mentally disabled due to a brain tumor. Along with his older brothers, his younger brothers also suffered from ailments. They were either deaf or tuberculosis patients, too. Four of the brothers died due to illnesses spread during the flu season. On top of all these problems, the boy was also abused.

Instead of giving up, this boy accepted his life in this unfortunate environment. All around him, life was dark, but he found pleasure in music. Music about love and hope soon became his support, acting as both parents and friends to him. Even though his life was tragic, he had blessed and amazing musical talent.

Throughout his life, his fate as a musician tortured him. Due to an illness, he developed some mental instability. This continuing illness that plagued his body disturbed his work as well as his emotions. In his head, he heard strange things such as knocking, scratching, and crying. Because of this illness, he eventually lost his hearing. In addition to his mental trouble, he had frequent headaches and abdominal pain that harassed him for over 30 years. Even though he suffered a lot, however, he still loved his music and people.

As a tribute to the talent that was given to him, he wrote an astonishing piece of music for an orchestra. This piece of music took five years to write, but even though it took a long time to write, it was short in nature, being only thirty minutes in length. We all have heard this celebrated music in some form. The music that has been described is Beethoven's 5th Symphony.

Even though plagued with a tragic life, Beethoven overcame his many troubles through his love and talent for music. He left one thrilling symphony for us all to enjoy. Together with his passion and patience, this extraordinary piece of music teaches us all about the lasting value of human life.

Story Writing Wings 02   Symphony

Writing Guideline

Writing Guideline

1 목적어와 보어

II Sentences with Grammar   p. 14

1. The volunteer became a representative.
2. The woman was the controller.
3. The student was smart.
4. The customers were picky.
5. Everybody accepted the suggestion.
6. People liked the taste.
7. The building has a big clock.
8. The itching tortured me.
9. The noises disturbed my concentration.
10. My brother made something.
11. A passenger lost his passport.
12. His scolding harassed the workers.
13. The art teacher prepared a piece of paper.
14. The construction took 11 years.
15. His speech was 28 seconds.
16. The participants listened to the news.
17. The view is sublime.
18. The challenger overcame his shortcomings.
19. Her last words left suggestiveness.
20. This book teaches the importance of exercise.

III Story Writing: Paragraph 1   p. 17

2 Sentence Writing

1. His father was an alcoholic.
2. His mother was a tuberculosis patient.
3. He had seven brothers.
4. His oldest brother was blind.
5. His second oldest brother had a mental disability.
6. His younger brothers were deaf and tuberculosis patients.
7. Four brothers died of diseases.
8. He was abused.

3 Paragraph Writing

> **Paragraph 1**
>
> His father was an alcoholic. His mother was a tuberculosis patient. He had seven brothers. His oldest brother was blind. His second oldest brother had a mental

disability. His younger brothers were deaf and tuberculosis patients. Four brothers died of diseases. He was abused.

IV Story Writing: Paragraph 2   p. 19

2 Sentence Writing

1. This boy accepted his fate.
2. His life was dark, but he liked music.
3. Music became his parents.
4. He had talent.
5. His fate tortured him.
6. He had mental troubles.
7. The illness disturbed his work.
8. He heard strange things.
9. He lost his hearing.
10. His headache and abdominal pain harassed him for 30 years.

3 Paragraph Writing

Paragraph 2

This boy accepted his fate. His life was dark, but he liked music. Music became his parents. He had talent. His fate tortured him. He had mental troubles. The illness disturbed his work. He heard strange things. He lost his hearing. His headache and abdominal pain harassed him for 30 years.

V Story Writing: Paragraph 3   p. 21

2 Sentence Writing

1. He loved music.
2. He loved people.
3. He wrote a piece of music.
4. The music took five years, but it was short.
5. The music was only 30 minutes long.
6. We listen to this piece of music every day.
7. It is Beethoven's 5th Symphony.
8. Beethoven had a tragic life, but he overcame his fate.
9. He left one symphony.
10. It teaches the value of life.

Writing Guideline

3 Paragraph Writing

Paragraph 3

He loved music. He loved people. He wrote a piece of music. The music took five years, but it was short. The music was only 30 minutes long. We listen to this piece of music every day. It is Beethoven's 5th Symphony. Beethoven had a tragic life, but he overcame his fate. He left one symphony, and it teaches the value of life.

VI Error Analysis p. 23

His father were (was) an alcoholic. His mother were (was) a tuberculosis patients (patient). He has (had) seven brothers. His oldest brother were (was) blind. His second oldest brother had a mental disability. His younger brothers was (were) deaf and tuberculosis patient (patients). Four brothers died of diseases. He was abuse (abused).

This boy except (accepted) his fate. His life was dark, but he liked music. Music become (became) his parents. He had talent. His fate tortured he (him). He have (had) mental troubles. The illness disturbed her (his) work. He heard strange things. He lost his hearing. His headache and abdominal pain harassed him in 30 year (for years).

He loved music. He loved peoples (people). He wrote a piece of a (삭제) music. The music took five years, but it is (was) short. A (The) music was only 30 minute (minutes) long. We listen (listen to) this piece of music every day. It is Beethoven's 5th Symphony. Beethoven had a tragic lives (life), but he overcome (overcame) his fate. He left one symphony. They teach (It teaches) the value of life.

2 형용사의 한정적 용법

II Sentences with Grammar p. 30

1. The volunteer became an **important** representative.
2. The woman was the **strict** controller.
3. The **new** student was smart.
4. The **foreign** customers were picky.
5. Everybody accepted the **reasonable** suggestion.

6. **Some** people liked the taste.
7. The building has a big and **gorgeous** clock.
8. The **severe** itching tortured me.
9. The **constant** noises disturbed my concentration.
10. My **smart** brother made something.
11. A **male** passenger lost his passport.
12. His **inquisitive** scolding harassed the workers.
13. The art teacher prepared a piece of **blue** paper.
14. The **dangerous** construction took 11 years.
15. His **powerful** speech was 28 seconds.
16. The participants listened to the **important** news.
17. The **breathtaking** view is sublime.
18. The **great** challenger overcame his shortcomings.
19. Her last words left **strong** suggestiveness.
20. This book teaches the **true** importance of exercise.

III Story Writing: Paragraph 1   p. 33

2 Sentence Writing

1. His **abusive** father was an alcoholic.
2. His mother was a **serious** tuberculosis patient.
3. He had seven brothers.
4. His oldest brother was **born** blind.
5. His second oldest brother had a mental disability.
6. His younger brothers were deaf and **fatal** tuberculosis patients.
7. Four brothers died of **incurable** diseases.
8. He was abused.

3 Paragraph Writing

Paragraph 1

His **abusive** father was an alcoholic. His mother was a **serious** tuberculosis patient. He had seven brothers. His oldest brother was **born** blind. His second oldest brother had a mental disability. His younger brothers were deaf and **fatal** tuberculosis patients. Four brothers died of **incurable** diseases. He was abused.

IV Story Writing: Paragraph 2   p. 35

2 Sentence Writing

1. This boy accepted his **unfortunate** fate.
2. His **difficult** life was dark, but he liked music.

Writing Guideline

3. Music became his **spiritual** parents.
4. He had **natural** talent.
5. His fate tortured him.
6. He had **severe** mental troubles.
7. The **constant** illness disturbed his work.
8. He heard strange things.
9. He lost his hearing.
10. His **painful** headache and abdominal pain harassed him for 30 years.

3 Paragraph Writing

Paragraph 2

This boy accepted his **unfortunate** fate. His **difficult** life was dark, but he liked music. Music became his **spiritual** parents. He had **natural** talent. His fate tortured him. He had **severe** mental troubles. The **constant** illness disturbed his work. He heard strange things. He lost his hearing. His **painful** headache and abdominal pain harassed him for 30 years.

V Story Writing: Paragraph 3   p. 37

2 Sentence Writing

1. He loved music.
2. He loved **all** people.
3. He wrote a piece of **powerful** music.
4. The music took five years, but it was short.
5. The **breathtaking** music was only 30 minutes long.
6. We listen to this piece of **sensational** music every day.
7. It is Beethoven's 5th Symphony.
8. Beethoven had a **tragic** life, but he overcame his fate.
9. He left one **sublime** symphony.
10. The **great** symphony teaches the **true** value of life.

3 Paragraph Writing

Paragraph 3

He loved music. He loved **all** people. He wrote a piece of **powerful** music. The music took five years, but it was short. The **breathtaking** music was only 30 minutes long. We listen to this piece of **sensational** music every day. It is Beethoven's 5th Symphony. Beethoven had a **tragic** life, but he overcame his fate. He left one **sublime** symphony. The **great** symphony teaches the **true** value of life.

VI. Error Analysis   p. 39

His abusive father was ~~alcoholic~~ [an alcoholic]. His mother was a serious tuberculosis ~~patients~~ [patient].
He had seven ~~brother~~ [brothers]. His oldest brother was ~~borned~~ [born] blind. His second oldest brother ~~was~~ [had] a mental disability. ~~He's~~ [His] younger brothers ~~was~~ [were] deaf and fatal tuberculosis patients. Four brothers ~~killed~~ [died] of ~~curable~~ [incurable] diseases. He was ~~abusive~~ [abused].
This boy accepted his ~~unfortunately~~ [unfortunate] fate. His difficult life was dark, ~~and~~ [but] he liked music. Music ~~becames~~ [became] his ~~spiritually~~ [spiritual] parents. He had ~~nature~~ [natural] talent. His fate tortured him. He ~~has~~ [had] severe mental troubles. The ~~consonant~~ [constant] illness disturbed his work. He heard strange things. He lost his ~~hear~~ [hearing]. His ~~a~~ [삭제] painful headache and ~~an~~ [an 삭제] abdominal pain harassed him ~~during~~ [for] 30 years.
He loved ~~a~~ [a 삭제] music. He loved all people. He wrote a ~~peace~~ [piece] of powerful music. The music ~~taken~~ [took] five years, but ~~he~~ [it] was short. The breathtaking music was only 30 minutes ~~longer~~ [long]. We listen to this piece of sensational music every day. It is Beethoven's 5th ~~symphony~~ [Symphony]. Beethoven had ~~tragic life~~ [a tragic life], but he ~~overcomes~~ [overcame] his fate. He left one sublime symphony. This great symphony teaches the true value ~~at~~ [of] life.

③ 현재분사와 과거분사

II. Sentences with Grammar   p. 42

1. The volunteer became a **supporting** representative.
2. The woman was the **scaring** controller.
3. The **selected** student was smart.
4. The **waiting** customers were picky.
5. Everybody accepted the **revised** suggestion.
6. The **invited** people liked the taste.
7. The building has a **glittering** and **dazzling** clock.
8. The **infected** itching tortured me.
9. The **continuing** noises disturbed my concentration.
10. My **educated** brother made something.
11. A **hurried** passenger lost his passport.

Writing Guideline

12 His **nagging** scolding harassed the workers.
13 The art teacher prepared a piece of **colored** paper.
14 The **tunneling** construction took 11 years.
15 His **touching** speech was 28 seconds.
16 The participants listened to the **surprising** news.
17 The **thrilling** view is sublime.
18 The **noted** challenger overcame his shortcomings.
19 Her last words left **baffling** suggestiveness.
20 This book teaches the **lasting** importance of exercise.

III Story Writing: Paragraph 1   p. 45

2 Sentence Writing

1 His abusive father was an alcoholic.
2 His mother was an **untreated** tuberculosis patient.
3 He had seven brothers.
4 His oldest brother was **suffered** blindness.
5 His second oldest brother had a mental disability.
6 His younger brothers were deaf and **infected** tuberculosis patients.
7 Four brothers died of **spreading** diseases.
8 He was **abused**.

3 Paragraph Writing

Paragraph 1

His abusive father was an alcoholic. His mother was an **untreated** tuberculosis patient. He had seven brothers. His oldest brother was **suffered** blindness. His second oldest brother had a mental disability. His younger brothers were deaf and **infected** tuberculosis patients. Four brothers died of **spreading** diseases. He was **abused**.

IV Story Writing: Paragraph 2   p. 47

2 Sentence Writing

1 This boy accepted his **saddened** fate.
2 His **troubled** life was dark, but he liked music.
3 Music became his **supporting** parents.
4 He had **blessed** talent.
5 His fate tortured him.
6 He had **distressing** mental troubles.

7 The **continuing** illness disturbed his work.
8 He heard strange things.
9 He lost his hearing.
10 His headache and abdominal pain harassed him for 30 years.

3 Paragraph Writing

Paragraph 2

This boy accepted his **saddened** fate. His **troubled** life was dark, but he liked music. Music became his **supporting** parents. He had **blessed** talent. His fate tortured him. He had **distressing** mental troubles. The **continuing** illness disturbed his work. He heard strange things. He lost his hearing. His headache and abdominal pain harassed him for 30 years.

V Story Writing: Paragraph 3   p. 49

2 Sentence Writing

1 He loved music.
2 He loved people.
3 He wrote a piece of **astonishing** music.
4 The music took five years, but it was short.
5 The **amazing** music was only 30 minutes long.
6 We listen to this piece of **celebrated** music every day.
7 It is Beethoven's 5th Symphony.
8 Beethoven had a tragic life, but he overcame his fate.
9 He left one **thrilling** symphony.
10 The **dignified** symphony teaches the **lasting** value of life.

3 Paragraph Writing

Paragraph 3

He loved music. He loved people. He wrote a piece of **astonishing** music. The music took five years, but it was short. The **amazing** music was only 30 minutes long. We listen to this piece of **celebrated** music every day. It is Beethoven's 5th Symphony. Beethoven had a tragic life, but he overcame his fate. He left one **thrilling** symphony. The **dignified** symphony teaches the **lasting** value of life.

Writing Guideline

VI Error Analysis p. 51

His abusive father was an alcoholic. His mother was an ~~intreated~~ tuberculosis
                                                        untreated
patient. He ~~has~~ seven brothers. His oldest brother was suffered blindness. His
            had
second oldest ~~brothers~~ had a ~~mantel~~ disability. His younger brothers ~~was~~ deaf and
              brother   mental   were
~~effected~~ tuberculosis patients. Four brothers ~~die~~ of spreading diseases. He was
infected   died
abused.

This boy accepted his saddened fate. His ~~traveled~~ life was ~~darks~~, but he liked
                                         troubled   dark
~~musics~~. Music ~~becam~~ his supporting parents. He had blessed talent. His fate
music   became
~~tutored~~ him. He had distressing mental troubles. The ~~counting~~ illness ~~disturb~~ his
tortured   continuing   disturbed
work. He heard strange things. He ~~losts~~ his hearing. His ~~headaches~~ and abdominal
                                  lost   headache
pain harassed him ~~per~~ 30 years.
                  for

He loved ~~a~~ music. He loved people. He ~~wrotes~~ a piece of ~~an~~ astonishing music.
         a 삭제   wrote   an 삭제
The music took five ~~ears~~, but it was ~~shorts~~. The amazing music was only 30
                    years   short
minutes ~~log~~. We ~~listen~~ this piece ~~over~~ celebrated music every day. It is ~~beethoven's~~
        long   listen to   of   Beethoven's
5th Symphony. Beethoven had ~~an~~ tragic life, but ~~she~~ overcame his fate. He left one
                            a   he
~~drilling~~ symphony. The ~~symphony dignified~~ teaches the lasting value of life.
thrilling   dignified symphony

④ 전치사구의 형용사적 용법

II Sentences with Grammar p. 54

1. The woman **in the office** was the scaring controller.
2. The selected student **through the vote** was smart.
3. The waiting customers **in line** were picky.
4. Everybody **as core members** accepted the revised suggestion.
5. The invited people **to the dinner party** liked the taste.
6. The building **across the street** has a glittering and dazzling clock.
7. The infected itching **on my skin** tortured me.
8. The continuing noises **outside the house** disturbed my concentration.
9. My educated brother **with me** made something.
10. A hurried passenger **in the airport** lost his passport.

11 His nagging scolding **over nothing** harassed the workers.
12 The art teacher **at school** prepared a piece of colored paper.
13 The tunneling construction **along the river** took 11 years.
14 His touching speech **before the opening ceremony** was only 28 seconds.
15 The participants **in the conference** listened to the surprising news.
16 The thrilling view **over the mountain** is sublime.
17 The noted challenger **in the competition** overcame his shortcomings.
18 Her last words **about peace** left baffling suggestiveness.
19 The book **of the year** teaches the lasting importance of exercise.

III Story Writing: Paragraph 1   p. 57

2 Sentence Writing

1 His father **at home** was an alcoholic.
2 His mother **in the bed** was an untreated tuberculosis patient.
3 He had seven brothers.
4 His oldest brother **with a genetic disease** was suffered blindness.
5 His second oldest brother **in the family** had a mental disability.
6 His younger brothers **inside the house** were deaf and infected tuberculosis patients.
7 Four brothers **among them** died of spreading diseases.
8 He was abused.

3 Paragraph Writing

Paragraph 1

His father **at home** was an alcoholic. His mother **in the bed** was an untreated tuberculosis patient. He had seven brothers. His oldest brother **with a genetic disease** was suffered blindness. His second oldest brother **in the family** had a mental disability. His younger brothers **inside the house** were deaf and infected tuberculosis patients. Four brothers **among them** died of spreading diseases. He was abused.

IV Story Writing: Paragraph 2   p. 59

2 Sentence Writing

1 This boy **under the unfortunate environment** accepted his saddened fate.
2 His troubled life **around him** was dark, but he liked music.
3 Music **about love and hope** became his supporting parents.
4 He had blessed talent.
5 His fate **as a musician** tortured him.

Writing Guideline

6. He had distressing mental troubles.
7. The continuing illness **in his body** disturbed his work.
8. He heard strange things.
9. He lost his hearing.
10. His headache and abdominal pain **during his work** harassed him for 30 years.

3 Paragraph Writing

Paragraph 2

This boy **under the unfortunate environment** accepted his saddened fate. His troubled life **around him** was dark, but he liked music. Music **about love and hope** became his supporting parents. He had blessed talent. His fate **as a musician** tortured him. He had distressing mental troubles. The continuing illness **in his body** disturbed his work. He heard strange things. He lost his hearing. His headache and abdominal pain **during his work** harassed him for 30 years.

V Story Writing: Paragraph 3   p. 61

2 Sentence Writing

1. He loved music. He loved people.
2. He wrote a piece of astonishing music **for an orchestra**.
3. The music took five years, but it was short.
4. The amazing music was only 30 minutes long.
5. We listen to this piece of celebrated music every day.
6. It is Beethoven's 5th Symphony.
7. Beethoven **with musical talent** had a tragic life.
8. He overcame his fate.
9. He left one thrilling symphony.
10. The dignified symphony **from his passion** teaches the lasting value of life.

3 Paragraph Writing

Paragraph 3

He loved music. He loved people. He wrote a piece of astonishing music **for an orchestra**. The music took five years, but it was short. The amazing music was only 30 minutes long. We listen to this piece of celebrated music every day. It is Beethoven's 5th Symphony. Beethoven **with musical talent** had a tragic life, but he overcame his fate. He left one thrilling symphony. The dignified symphony **from his passion** teaches the lasting value of life.

VI. Error Analysis   p. 63

His father at home was an alcoholic. His mother ~~in bed~~ was ~~untreated~~ tuberculosis
                                              in the bed   *an untreated*
patient. ~~She~~ had seven brothers. His oldest brother ~~for~~ a genetic disease was
         He   *with*
suffered blindness. His second oldest brother in the family ~~head~~ a mental disability.
                                                             had
His younger brothers ~~side~~ the house were deaf and infected tuberculosis ~~patient~~.
                     inside   *patients*
Four ~~brother~~ among ~~their~~ died of spreading diseases. He was ~~abusing~~.
     brothers   *them*   *abused*
This boy under the ~~fortunate~~ environment accepted his saddened fate. ~~He's~~
                   unfortunate   *His*
troubled life ~~round~~ him ~~were~~ dark, but he liked music. ~~A music above~~ love and
              around   *was*   *Music   about*
hope became his ~~supported~~ parents. He had blessed talent. His fate as ~~musician~~
                supporting   *a musician*
tortured ~~himself~~. He had distressing mental troubles. The ~~continued~~ illness in his
         him   *continuing*
body disturbed his ~~walk~~. He heard strange ~~thinks~~. He lost his hearing. His headache
                   work   *things*
and abdominal pain during his work harassed him for 30 years.

He ~~love~~ music. He loved people. He ~~writted~~ a piece of ~~an~~ astonishing music for
   loved   *wrote*   *an 삭제*
an orchestra. The music took five years, but it was ~~shutter~~. The amazing music was
                                                    short
only 30 ~~minuets~~ long. We listen to this piece of celebrated music every day. It ~~was~~
        minutes   *is*
~~Beethovens~~ 5th Symphony. Beethoven ~~beyond~~ musical talent had a tragic life, but
Beethoven's   *with*
he ~~over came~~ his fate. He ~~lefted~~ one thrilling symphony. The ~~dignifying~~ symphony
   overcame   *left*   *dignfied*
about his passion teaches the ~~lasted~~ value of life.
from   *lasting*

5 합성전치사

II. Sentences with Grammar   p. 66

1. The volunteer became a supporting representative **in the course of** the meeting.
2. The selected student through the vote was smart **on the part** of the class management.
3. The customers were picky **in comparison with** others.
4. Everybody accepted the revised suggestion **because of** its simplicity.
5. The invited people to the dinner party liked the taste **in addition to** the sweet smell.
6. The building across the street has a glittering and dazzling clock **on top of** the roof.

Writing Guideline

7. The infected itching on my skin tortured me **together with** ooze.
8. The continuing noises disturbed my concentration **as well as** my sleep.
9. My brother made something **out of** it.
10. A passenger in the airport lost his passport **along with** his briefcase.
11. His nagging scolding harassed the workers **next to** him.
12. The art teacher prepared a piece of colored paper **instead of** plain paper.
13. The tunneling construction took 11 years **because of** its difficulties.
14. The participants in the conference listened to the surprising news **in regard to** the schedule.
15. The thrilling view is sublime **in spite of** the bad weather.
16. The challenger in the competition overcame his shortcomings **instead of** giving up.
17. Her last words about peace left baffling suggestiveness **alongside of** a question.

III Story Writing: Paragraph 1   p. 69

2 Sentence Writing

1. His father at home was an alcoholic **as a result of** heavy drinking.
2. His mother in the bed was an untreated tuberculosis patient.
3. He had seven brothers.
4. His oldest brother with a genetic disease was confirmed blind.
5. His second oldest brother in the family had a mental disability **because of** the brain tumor.
6. His younger brothers inside the house were deaf and infected tuberculosis patients.
7. Four brothers among them died of spreading diseases **in connection with** the flu.
8. He was abused.

3 Paragraph Writing

Paragraph 1

His father at home was an alcoholic **as a result of** heavy drinking. His mother in the bed was an untreated tuberculosis patient. He had seven brothers. His oldest brother with a genetic disease was confirmed blind. His second oldest brother in the family had a mental disability **because of** the brain tumor. His younger brothers inside the house were deaf and infected tuberculosis patients. Four brothers among them died of spreading diseases **in connection with** the flu. He was abused.

IV Story Writing: Paragraph 2   p. 71

2 Sentence Writing

1. This boy under the unfortunate environment accepted his saddened fate **instead**

of giving up.
2. His troubled life around him was dark, but he liked music.
3. Music about love and hope became his supporting parents **as well as** friends.
4. He had blessed talent **in contrast to** his tragic life.
5. His fate as a musician tortured him **in the course of** his life.
6. He had mental troubles **due to** the illness.
7. The continuing illness in his body disturbed his work **as well as his emotion**.
8. He heard strange things **such as** knocking, scratching, and crying.
9. He lost his hearing **because of** this illness.
10. His headache and abdominal pain during his work harassed him for 30 years **in addition to** his mental troubles.

3 Paragraph Writing

Paragraph 2

This boy under the unfortunate environment accepted his saddened fate **instead of giving up**. His troubled life around him was dark, but he liked music. Music about love and hope became his supporting parents **as well as** friends. He had blessed talent **in contrast to** his tragic life. His fate as a musician tortured him **in the course of his life**. He had mental troubles **due to** the illness. The continuing illness in his body disturbed his work **as well as his emotion**. He heard strange things **such as knocking, scratching, and crying**. He lost his hearing **because of this illness**. His headache and abdominal pain during his work harassed him for 30 years **in addition to** his mental troubles.

V Story Writing: Paragraph 3 p. 75

2 Sentence Writing

1. He loved music **in spite of** this suffering.
2. He loved people **in spite of** this pain.
3. He wrote a piece of astonishing music for an orchestra **in return for** his talent.
4. The music for people took five years.
5. The music was short **in terms of** the playing time.
6. The music was only 30 minutes long.
7. We listen to this piece of celebrated music every day.
8. It is Beethoven's 5th Symphony.
9. Beethoven with musical talent had a tragic life.
10. He overcame his fate inside him. He left one thrilling symphony.
11. The dignified symphony from his fate teaches the lasting value of life **together with** his passion and patience.

Writing Guideline

3 Paragraph Writing

Paragraph 3

He loved music **in spite of** this suffering. He loved people **in spite of** this pain. He wrote a piece of astonishing music for an orchestra **in return for** his talent. The music for people took five years, but it was short **in terms of** the playing time. The music was only 30 minutes long. We listen to this piece of celebrated music every day. It is Beethoven's 5th Symphony. Beethoven with musical talent had a tragic life, but he overcame the fate inside him. He left one thrilling symphony. The dignified symphony from his fate teaches the lasting value of life **together with** his passion and patience.

VI Error Analysis   p. 77

His father at a home was an alcoholic ~~as result of~~ heavy drinking. His mother in
        a 삭제   a result

the bed was an ~~untreating~~ tuberculosis ~~patience~~. He had seven brothers. His oldest
         untreated   patient

brother with a genetic disease was confirmed blind. His second oldest brother in

the family had a mental disability ~~because~~ the brain tumor. His younger brothers
              because of

inside the house were deaf and infected tuberculosis patients. Four brothers among

them ~~dying~~ of the spreading diseases ~~in contact with~~ the flu. He was abused.
   died   in contrast to

This boy under the unfortunate environment accepted his saddened fate ~~instead off~~
                                                    instead of

giving up. His troubled life ~~among~~ him was dark, but he liked music. Music about
               around

love and a hope ~~be came~~ his supporting parents as well as friends. He had blessed
    a 삭제   became

talent in contrast ~~for~~ his tragic life. His fate as a ~~magician~~ tortured him in ~~course~~
            to   musician   the course

of his life. He had mental troubles due to ~~illness~~. The continuing illness in ~~its~~ body
            the illness   his

disturbed ~~its~~ work as well as his ~~motion~~. He heard strange things such as knocking,
 his   emotion

scratching, ~~crying~~. He lost his hearing ~~because~~ this illness. His ~~head ache~~ and
   and crying   because of   headache

abdominal pain during his work harassed him ~~from~~ 30 years in ~~addition~~ his mental
                                 for   addition to

troubles.

He loved music ~~despite of~~ this suffering. He loved people in spite of this pain.
    in spite of

He ~~written~~ a piece of astonishing music for an orchestra in ~~return~~ his talent. The
  wrote   return for

music of people took five year, but it was short in terms for the playing time. The
    for   years   of
music was only 30 minutes long. We listen to this piece of celebrated music every
day. It's Beethoven's 5th Symphony. Beethoven for talent musical had a tragic life,
                                              with musical talent
but he overcame the fate inside him. He left one thrilling symphony. A dignified
                                                                              The
symphony form his fate teaches the lasting value of life together over his passion
         from   with
and patient.
    patience

❻ 합성전치사의 강조

Ⅱ Sentences with Grammar   p. 80

1. **On the part of** the class management, the selected student through the vote was smart.
2. **In comparison with** others, the customers were picky.
3. **Because of** its simplicity, everybody accepted the revised suggestion.
4. **In the course of** the meeting, the volunteer became a supporting representative.
5. **In addition to** the sweet smell, the invited people to the dinner party liked the taste.
6. **On top of** the roof, the building across the street has a glittering and dazzling clock.
7. **Along with** his briefcase, a passenger in the airport lost his passport.
8. **Instead of** plain paper, the art teacher prepared a piece of colored paper.
9. **Because of** its difficulties, the tunneling construction took 11 years.
10. **In contrast to** other long speech, his touching speech before the opening ceremony was 28 seconds.
11. **In regard to** the schedule, the participants in the conference listened to the surprising news.
12. **In spite of** the bad weather, the thrilling view is sublime.
13. **Instead of** giving up, the challenger in the competition overcame his shortcomings.
14. **Alongside of** a question, her last words about peace left baffling suggestiveness.

Ⅲ Story Writing: Paragraph 1   p. 83

2 Sentence Writing

1. <u>**As a result of** heavy drinking</u>, his father at home was an alcoholic.
2. His mother in the bed was an untreated tuberculosis patient.
3. He had seven brothers.

Writing Guideline

4. His oldest brother with a genetic disease was confirmed blind.
5. **Because of** the brain tumor, his second oldest brother in the family had a mental disability.
6. His younger brothers inside the house were deaf and infected tuberculosis patients.
7. **In connection with** the flu, four brothers among them died of spreading diseases.
8. He was abused.

3 Paragraph Writing

Paragraph 1

As a result of heavy drinking, his father at home was an alcoholic. His mother in the bed was an untreated tuberculosis patient. He had seven brothers. His oldest brother with a genetic disease was confirmed blind. **Because of** the brain tumor, his second oldest brother in the family had a mental disability. His younger brothers inside the house were deaf and infected tuberculosis patients. **In connection with the flu**, four brothers among them died of spreading diseases. He was abused.

IV Story Writing: Paragraph 2   p. 85

2 Sentence Writing

1. **Instead of** giving up, this boy accepted his fate under the unfortunate environment.
2. His troubled life around him was dark, but he liked music.
3. Music about love and hope became his supporting parents **as well as** friends.
4. **In contrast to** his tragic life, he had blessed talent.
5. **In the course of** his life, his fate as a musician tortured him.
6. **Due to** the illness, he had mental troubles.
7. The continuing illness in his body disturbed his work **as well as** his emotion.
8. In his head, he heard strange things **such as** knocking, scratching, and crying.
9. **Because of** this illness, he lost his hearing.
10. **In addition to** his mental troubles, his headache and abdominal pain during his work harassed him for 30 years.

3 Paragraph Writing

Paragraph 2

Instead of giving up, this boy accepted his fate under the unfortunate environment. His troubled life around him was dark, but he liked music. Music about love and hope became his supporting parents **as well as** friends. **In contrast to his tragic life**, he had blessed talent. **In the course of his life**, his fate as a musician tortured him. **Due to** the illness, he had mental troubles. The continuing illness in his body disturbed his work **as well as his emotion**. He heard strange things **such as**

knocking, scratching, and crying. **Because of** this illness, he lost his hearing. **In addition to** his mental troubles, his headache and abdominal pain during his work harassed him for 30 years.

V Story Writing: Paragraph 3   p. 87

2 Sentence Writing

1. **In spite of** this suffering, he loved music.
2. **In spite of** this pain, he loved people.
3. **In return for** his talent, he wrote a piece of astonishing music for an orchestra.
4. The music for people took five years, but **in terms of** the playing time, it was short.
5. The music was only 30 minutes long.
6. We listen to this piece of celebrated music every day.
7. It is Beethoven's 5th Symphony.
8. **Along with** musical talent, he had a tragic life, but he overcame the fate inside him.
9. He left one thrilling symphony.
10. **Together with** his passion and patience, this dignified symphony from his fate teaches the lasting value of life.

3 Paragraph Writing

Paragraph 3

In spite of this suffering, he loved music. **In spite of** this pain, he loved people. **In return for** his talent, he wrote a piece of astonishing music for an orchestra. The music for people took five years, but **in terms of** the playing time, it was short. The music was only 30 minutes long. We listen to this piece of celebrated music every day. It is Beethoven's 5th Symphony. **Along with** musical talent, he had a tragic life, but he overcame the fate inside him. He left one thrilling symphony. **Together with** his passion and patience, this dignified symphony from his fate teaches the lasting value of life.

VI Error Analysis   p. 89

As the ~~result~~ of heavy drinking, his father at home was an ~~alcoholics~~. His mother
    a   *alcoholic*
in the bed was an untreated tuberculosis patient. He had ~~sevens~~ brothers. His oldest
                                                                            seven
brother with a ~~genet~~ disease was confirmed ~~blinder~~. ~~Because~~ the brain tumor, his
                  genetic   *blind* *Because of*
second oldest ~~brothers~~ in the family had a mental disability. His younger brothers
                       brother

Writing Guideline

inside the house ~~wore deafs~~ [were deaf] and infected tuberculosis patients. ~~For~~ [In] connection with the flu, four brothers among them died of the ~~spraying~~ [spreading] diseases. He was abused. ~~In stead~~ [Instead] of giving up, this boy accepted his fate under a unfortunate environment [the]. His troubled life around him was ~~dark but~~ [dark, but], he liked music. Music about ~~loves~~ [love] and ~~hopes~~ [hope] became his supporting ~~parentals~~ [parents] as ~~will~~ [well] as friends. ~~Incontrast~~ [In contrast] to his tragic life, he had blessed talent. In the ~~courses~~ [course] of his life, his fate as a musician tortured him. Due ~~of~~ [to] the illness, he had mental troubles. The continuing illness in his body ~~disrobed~~ [disturbed] his work ~~well~~ [as well] as his emotion. He heard strange things such as ~~knockings~~ [knocking], scratching, and crying. ~~Be cause~~ [Because] of this illness, he lost his hearing. In addition ~~for~~ [to] his mental troubles, his headache and abdominal pain during ~~work his~~ [his work] harassed him for 30 ~~year's~~ [years]. ~~Inspite~~ [In spite] of this suffering, he loved music. In spite of this ~~painless~~ [pain], he loved people. In ~~returning~~ [return] for his talent, he wrote a piece of ~~estonishing~~ [astonishing] music for an orchestra. The music for people took five years, but in ~~term~~ [terms] of the ~~playtime~~ [playing time], it was short. The music was only 30 minutes. We listen to this piece of celebrated music every day.

It is ~~Beethovens'~~ [Beethoven's] 5th Symphony. ~~Long~~ [Along] with ~~magical~~ [musical] talent, he had a ~~traffic~~ [tragic] life, but he ~~is~~ [삭제] overcame the fate inside him. He left one thrilling symphony. ~~All together~~ [Together] with his passion and patience, this dignified symphony from his fate teaches the lasting value of life.